THE
BROTHERS DALZIEL

A RECORD OF WORK · 1840–1890

Foreword by
GRAHAM REYNOLDS

Reprinted by
B. T. BATSFORD LTD · LONDON

ORIGINALLY PUBLISHED 1901
THIS EDITION : 1978
FOREWORD © GRAHAM REYNOLDS
PRINTED IN GREAT BRITAIN BY
BUTLER & TANNER LIMITED
FROME, WILTSHIRE

ISBN 0 7134 1530 4

FOREWORD

The Brothers Dalziel tells the story of one of the most varied and successful establishments for wood engraving ever set up in England. It embodies the reminiscences of two old men – George Dalziel was 86 and Edward was 84 when it was published – who could look back on virtually the whole of the Victorian age and who realised, without rancour, that their craft had been superseded by process engraving. The period covered by their story has always been regarded as one of the richest in English book illustration. Wood engraving was not, of course, the only, nor always the dominant reproductive medium in use in the nineteenth century. Turner's vignettes for Roger's *Italy* and *Poems*, the finest illustrations produced during the 1830s, were rendered with marvellous delicacy in steel engraving. The earlier novels of Charles Dickens were mostly illustrated by the etched line of Cruikshank and 'Phiz'. Even more remarkably, John Martin found that the most expressive medium for the transmission of his apocalyptic visions of Hell and Judgment was the mezzotint, with its unrivalled capacity for intense blacks and subtly graded half-tones.

Yet wood engraving outstripped these methods in popularity throughout the middle years of the nineteenth century. It was found to be convenient for books and periodicals with long runs, since the wood block could be fitted into the text as though it were another piece of type. Then again, it was in tune with the stylistic changes which influenced the making of illustrative drawings in the early Victorian age. Those influences had largely come from Germany and involved a greater emphasis on line as opposed to tone. Such followers of the Nazarenes as Moritz Retzsch and Eduard von Bendemann had a strong effect on Daniel Maclise, and these influences culminated in the early drawings of the Pre-Raphaelites. It was fortunate that a whole body of craftsmen distinct from the line engravers, etchers, and lithographers was available to interpret a new type of design which depended more on outline than on crosshatching, shading and the other tonal devices. These workers in wood were the living heirs of the Bewick tradition.

When Thomas Bewick published his *History of Quadrupeds* (1790) and *History of British Birds* (1797, 1804), he did more than produce a classic series of natural history illustrations and vignettes of country life from his own designs. In the wake of their success he established a school of wood engravers centred on Newcastle-upon-Tyne. Subsequently many of his pupils set off for London, where the more intensive publishing activity of the metropolis gave greater opportunities for the practice of their craft. The strongly regional origin of these wood engravers is most striking. William Harvey, Charles Gray and Ebenezer Landells, who figure in the following account, were all born in Newcastle-upon-Tyne. The Dalziels tell a number of affectionate anecdotes about Landells; to them may be added the fact that he retained his Tyneside accent so thoroughly that he was known as 'Tooch it oop'. The Dalziels were geographically linked with these pioneers through their birthplace in Wooler, Northumberland and their subsequent home in Newcastle-upon-Tyne. When they came to London, it was from the Tyneside expatriates that they learnt wood engraving. The history they give of their apprenticeship shows how vital was the teaching of Bewick's pupils for the existence of a group of skilled wood engravers in the middle years of the nineteenth century.

But, by the time the Dalziels came to practise their craft, it was being used with a different stylistic accent from that of its originators. Bewick composed in tone rather than line. His wood blocks started as chunky adumbrations of an animal or a genre scene; he achieved definition by introducing white into the predominating black of the imprint, and tone by lowering the surface of his block. By the 1840s the balance between white and black had been reversed. The design was created in the block as it had been in the drawing, that is by creating black outlines or hatchings on an initially white space.

Much of the patronage for the draughtsmen and wood engravers of the Victorian age came from the illustrated periodicals which appeared in increasing quantities during the 1840s and subsequent decades. These publications encompassed a wide range of interest and of quality, ranging as they did from *The Penny Magazine* to the *People's Police Gazette*, and from *Punch* to the *Illustrated London News*. The Brothers Dalziel naturally do not dwell extensively on their commitments to the weekly press, preferring to stake their claim for the recognition of posterity on the work they did for 'fine art books'. As they record, conditions of work for the periodical press were not conducive to the control of quality. 'Drawings came to us on a Saturday evening, and we were compelled to deliver the engraved blocks to the printers on the Monday morning'. So stringent a deadline could only be met by dividing the wood block and employing several engravers on individual sections throughout the night. It is no surprise that work produced by many hands in this haste was often defective in quality. It has been suggested that much of the adverse criticism which was showered upon Millais's 'Christ in the House of his Parents' was evoked by the inadequate woodcut of the painting published in the *Illustrated London News* to accompany its review of the Royal Academy's exhibition for 1850. Certainly the defects in its drawing would go some way to account for the near hysteria of Dickens's tirade: 'supposing it were possible for any creature to exist for a moment with that dislocated throat . . . the kneeling woman, so horrible in her ugliness . . . the dirty drunkard in a high state of varicose veins'.

As the Dalziels freely admit, they were not the only firm of highly skilled wood engravers working in the Victorian age. It would be a difficult and unrewarding task to attempt to distinguish, on grounds of style alone, between two unsigned proofs, one from Dalziel, the other from Swain. Some artists preferred to be reproduced by John Thompson, Orrin Smith, W. J. Linton or Ebenezer Landells. What gives the Dalziels their special place of importance is the degree to which they became involved in the whole cycle of book production. They did not act solely as engravers of other people's designs. Seven of the eight sons of Alexander Dalziel were professional artists, and the plates in this book include illustrations by Thomas, Edward and Edward's son, E. G. Dalziel. In addition they became pioneers of a new method of publication, whereby the engraver acted as publisher, selecting both the subject of the book and the artists who were to design the cuts. In this capacity they acted as talent scouts, and it was one of their more significant contributions to the artistic patronage of their times that they were amongst the first to recognise the capabilities of the relatively unknown newcomers J. D. Watson, Fred Walker, G. J. Pinwell and J. W. North.

The establishment of the Camden Press in 1857 set the seal on their activities as printers and publishers. Before they embarked on these initiatives they had worked for some of the older and best established artists of the century. William Mulready was the finest draughtsman of the human figure working in early Victorian England. His classic designs for Goldsmith's *Vicar Of Wakefield* were engraved on wood by John Thompson in 1843. However, the Dalziels were asked in 1856 to engrave one of Mulready's drawings as an illustration to a poem by John Constable's friend the Rev. T. J. Judkin. The resulting block, 'Sleeping Child and Lamb' (p. 29) is one of their most delicate and sensitive cuts. Indeed, it is evident from the illustrations 'Threnody' (p 121) and 'The Battle-field' (p. 181) that Mulready had a strong influence on Edward Dalziel's designs. Amongst the other artists for whom they worked in the earlier stages of their career were W. E. Frost, John Tenniel and F. R. Pickersgill, whose reputation as an anticipator of the Pre-Raphaelites is perhaps justified by the illustration to Tennyson's 'Oriana' reproduced on p. 57. Sir John Gilbert's 'Lear fantastically dressed with flowers' (p. 79) is one of the memorable images created by this most prolific of illustrators, whose facility was such that he is said to have sent his large blocks in separate pieces to the engraver, not seeing the whole design till it had been cut. His speed of execution was in stark contrast to Richard Doyle's habits of procrastination. Yet, as his 'An Overland Journey to the Great Exhibition of 1851' (p. 60) shows, the work Doyle did succeed in accomplishing was delicate and highly original.

Percy Muir, whose *Victorian Illustrated Books* (1971) gives a balanced and comprehensive survey of the whole subject, entitles his chapter on the years 1855–1870 'The Dalziel Era'. Though, as we have seen, there were other engravers and other publishers, the description hardly exaggerates the firm's importance in this seminal epoch. The period, which is more frequently referred to as 'The Sixties', has a special character in English book illustration. In those years were published the greater part of the illustrated books which are eagerly collected and have been comprehensively charted in two studies: Gleeson White's *English Illustration: The Sixties* (1903) and Forrest Reid's *Illustrators of the Eighteen-Sixties* (1928). Both these writers depend for much of their information on the first-hand account given in *The Brothers Dalziel*. Muir places it as a source beside the two monographs by White and Reid, adding that this is 'despite its gossipy character, its irregular arrangement and its inadequate index'. All these faults the book has, yet its anecdotal tone is part of its charm, and it remains indispensible.

The period thus known as 'The Sixties' begins confusingly enough with a book published in 1855: William Allingham's *The Music Master* with illustrations designed by Rossetti, Millais and Arthur Hughes. When this was followed two years later by Moxon's edition of Tennyson's Poems, the Pre-Raphaelites' style emerged as the new force in illustration: original, clear, poetical and well adapted to the texts. The Dalziels made all the cuts for *The Music Master*, but they only executed 15 of the 54 illustrations for Moxon's *Tennyson*. For obvious reasons Millais is accorded the central place in the Dalziels' account of these years. Even so, their description of the *Tennyson*, which bulks so imposingly in the artistic history of those times, is incomplete. Moxon had engaged nine artists in all to design the illustrations for a work which he intended to be a monument both to Tennyson and to the art of his period. Five of the artists were long-established representatives of the old guard: Mulready, Creswick, Maclise, Stanfield and Horsley. The remaining four were first generation Pre-Raphaelites: Rossetti, Hunt, Millais, together with Woolner, who contributed a portrait medallion of Tennyson for engraving as the frontispiece.

The impression given by the correspondence they quote and their reflections upon it, that there was virtually a love feast between Millais and Dalziel, is not a misleading one. A number of other letters between the artist and the engraver have recently been published[1], and confirm the smooth and confiding relationship which developed between them. The meticulous attention to fine detail and his instinct for the engraver's difficulties is apparent in Millais's proof corrections and his allied correspondence with the Dalziels. The manuscript printed in facsimile on pp. 84–85[2] is typical in the emphasis it places on the correction of line and the elimination of unnecessary shadow, both important for the vital element of facial expression.

The happy working partnership between artist and engraver continued over a number of years and culminated in Millais's illustrations to Trollope's novels. These had the unusual distinction of pleasing the author as well. Trollope's praise was particularly heartfelt, since he incorporated it in his posthumously published autobiography: 'I do not think that more conscientious work was done by any man. . . . In every figure that he drew it was his object to promote the views of the writer whose works he had undertaken to illustrate, and he never spared himself any pains in studying that work, so as to enable him to do so. I have carried on some of those characters from book to book, and have had my own early ideas impressed indelibly on my memory by the excellence of his delineations.' Certainly the illustrations are cut with a facility which preserves the graphic freedom of the original drawings. But they show a more mundane aspect of Millais's talent than the medievalist reconstructions with which he made his mark as a rising young Pre-Raphaelite. Here Millais shows himself a keen and committed observer of contemporary social life. He followed his more poetic vein for Dalziel's project *Parables of Our Lord* but it took him six years to produce the twenty drawings with which it was eventually issued. Once again Millais is unstinting in his praise of Dalziel's cutting: 'Nothing can be more exquisitely rendered than the "Importunate Widow".' (p. 100).

Rossetti felt no such enthusiasm for their work. *The Brothers Dalziel* is so full of

[1] 'Letters from Sir John Everett Millais, Bart, P.R.A. (1829–1896) and William Holman Hunt, O.M. (1827–1910) in the Henry E. Huntington Library, San Marino, California' edited by Mary Lutyens, Walpole Society, Vol. XLIV, 1972–1974.
[2] Mary Lutyens, *loc. cit.*, gives a complete transcript and set of reproductions of the six pages of the letter of 15th February 1856 of which only the last two are reproduced in facsimile here.

quotations from satisfied clients that it is necessary, as a slight corrective to the almost monotonously laudatory tone, to reprint Rossetti's 'Address to Dalziel Brothers':

O woodman spare that block,
O gash not anyhow!
It took ten days by clock,
I'd fain preserve it now.

Chorus – *Wild laughter from Dalziels' Workshop.*

Again he wrote: 'These engravers! What ministers of wrath! Your drawing comes to them, like Agag, delicately, and is hewn to pieces before the Lord Harry. I took more pains with one block lately than I had done with anything for a long while. It came back to me on paper, the other day, with Dalziel performing his cannibal jig in the corner, and I have really felt like an invalid ever since.'

It is small wonder that the Dalziels' references to Rossetti are decidedly reserved in tone, and that they defend themselves from his strictures by saying that he had not mastered the art of drawing for the engraver. Since Rossetti found it hard enough to please himself, it was scarcely likely that another hand working over his designs would satisfy him. Yet in spite of these imperfect sympathies it is probable that the Dalziels' prints after such drawings by Rossetti as 'St. Cecillia' (p. 91) and 'The Maids of Elfenmere' gave many people their first real insight into the poetry of the Pre-Raphaelite movement. Burne-Jones thought the latter 'the most beautiful drawing for an illustration I have ever seen' and it encouraged him to devote himself to the practice of art.

The Dalziels reproduce here (pp. 161, 163) two of the drawings they cut from Burne-Jones's designs. It is interesting to find that the force of his dedication to other-worldly medievalism has caused them to deviate for once from their customary linear manner. In its place we find a tonal quality and black solidity which points forward to the publications of the Kelmscott Press. Other artists influenced by the Pre-Raphaelites were able to work more in accord with the established principles of the wood engravers. Frederick Sandys's moving illustration 'The Little Mourner' (p. 173) shows a perfect understanding of the medium in which the drawing is to be cut.

Although the Dalziels may have been concerned in only a relatively small proportion of the vast output of Victorian illustrated books, their work embodies the rich variety of subject matter which enthralled the growing reading public. It includes many reprints of well-tried classics, such as their *Don Quixote* illustrated by Houghton, and *Robinson Crusoe* illustrated by J. D. Watson. Of the perennial *Pilgrim's Progress* they produced at least four editions: William Harvey's of 1850, that illustrated by the 'new man' J. D. Watson, published in 1861, another by Thomas Dalziel, published two years later, and a fourth of 1880, in which a younger generation led by Fred Barnard played the most important part. A new departure was found in the publication of illustrations in which the landscape takes precedence over the figures. This was especially the province of Birket Foster, another Tynesider; the fact that he made 'literally no progress' as an apprentice in wood engraving with Landells did not prevent his staggering success as a watercolour painter, and the abortive training doubtless contributed to his ability to design intelligibly for the engraver (p. 145). The natural history illustration was another specialised form, of which Joseph Wolf was the acknowledged master (p. 269).

Domestic sentiment bulks large in an age characterised by moral rectitude, a heavy death rate amongst children and the uninhibited display of emotion on the part of men as well as women. Houghton's 'Kiss me' (p. 159), Fred Walker's 'A Woman in the Snow' (p. 199), and Pinwell's 'The Ballad Maker' (p. 215) are representative comments on the joys and sorrows of daily life. In this vein J. D. Watson's 'Abject Prayer' (p. 169) – when originally published in *London Society* it was called 'Ash Wednesday – is an archetypal expression of those agonies of the personal conscience which are so predominant a theme in the Victorian novel.

In complete contrast to these realistic scenes of domestic life were the exotics. The ever increasing desire for accuracy in Biblical illustration sent Wilkie, Roberts, Holman Hunt and many other artists out to the Near East to study its sites, manners and costumes. The fruits of this effort were soon apparent in the anthologies of stories from the Bible, to which the Dalziels made important contributions with Millais's *Parables of Our Lord* and the *Bible Gallery*. The same taste for oriental subject matter is given even freer scope in their 'Arabian Nights' in which Houghton displayed such mastery.

Of all illustrated books those produced for children have the longest active life. The work of Beatrix Potter and Ernest Shephard delights boys and girls today as it did their grandparents and great grandparents. The Dalziels entered this magic world when they re-engraved Edward Lear's *Book of Nonsense*, and they made sure of their enduring fame when they cut Tenniel's designs for *Alice in Wonderland* and *Through the Looking-Glass*. The 'cannibal jig' of their signature may be unnoticed, but these two books have introduced the Dalziels' name into countless nurseries. *Alice* is frequently reprinted, and it is only fitting that the Dalziels' history of their life's work, in which that publication was just an episode, should also now be reprinted. It is a first-hand account of a busy, active and talented artistic circle, an anthology of admirable engravings, and a characteristic embodiment of their ideas of book production.

Graham Reynolds

THE BROTHERS DALZIEL

A RECORD OF FIFTY YEARS' WORK

1840—1890

THE
BROTHERS DALZIEL

A RECORD

OF

FIFTY YEARS' WORK IN CONJUNCTION WITH
MANY OF THE MOST DISTINGUISHED
ARTISTS OF THE PERIOD
1840—1890

*WITH SELECTED PICTURES BY, AND AUTOGRAPH
LETTERS*

FROM

LORD LEIGHTON, P.R.A.,

SIR J. E. MILLAIS, BART., P.R.A., SIR E. J. POYNTER, P.R.A.,
HOLMAN HUNT, DANTE G. ROSSETTI, SIR JOHN TENNIEL,
SIR E. BURNE-JONES, BART., JOHN RUSKIN,

AND MANY OTHERS.

LONDON

METHUEN AND CO.

36 ESSEX STREET W.C.

1901

LONDON :

PRINTED BY DALZIEL AND CO., LTD.

CAMDEN PRESS, 110 HIGH STREET, CAMDEN TOWN.

PREFACE.

THOMAS BEWICK, who revived the art of wood engraving in England, was apprenticed to Ralph Beilby, as a copperplate engraver, in 1767. About 1770 he began to engrave on wood. The work at first was rough, and chiefly for newspaper advertisements; but he soon saw the capabilities of the material, and he rapidly developed into the great master of his art. The excellence of his wood engraving may be said to have culminated in his " Book of British Birds," the first volume of which was published in 1797. For a century from that date the art of wood engraving has been the most popular as well as the best method for the reproduction of all classes of drawings, and during that hundred years much beautiful work has been done.

Bewick's pupils were all artists in the fullest meaning of the word—John Bewick (his brother), Robert Johnson, Luke Clenell, Charlton Nesbit, Isaac Nicholson, and William Harvey. What a grand start the first half of the century of wood engraving had with such great men !

In the second half—in which we claim to have had our share—were such brilliant contemporaries as John Jackson, John Thomson, the Williams's,

J. W. Whymper, Orrin Smith, Mason Jackson, W. L. Thomas, W. J. Linton, J. D. Cooper, C. Roberts, Biscombe Gardner, Joseph Swain, and J. W. Palmer—all true artists, draughtsmen, and painters, as well as wood engravers.

Touching the old cry of defective reproduction, we say that at times there could not fail to be some amount of depreciation, but never such as justified the senseless and vulgar remarks made by certain critics, which can only be passed over in consideration of their total want of technical knowledge of the art, and of the conditions under which much of the work was produced. Coarse epithets have been used towards men who were devoting, with all possible earnestness, their skill to an art for the reproduction of work for popular issues. Wood engraving, being no exception to other arts, demands conditions necessary for the production of perfect work. First, the man who makes the drawing ought to know the capabilities of the material and should work accordingly; second, the engraver should have all the true instincts of an artist; and, third, he must have the full interval of time to perform his work with proper care.

A large amount of wood engraving being done on the rush, it was a common thing to "burn the midnight oil" and the engraver's eyes at the same time, and it is a marvel that so much beautiful artistic work was done under such conditions.

We have printed in this book many letters from distinguished artists expressing their satisfaction with our rendering of their drawings, with one object—to place beyond all doubt that if wood engravings were produced under the conditions named, the results would always prove satisfactory.

We have a letter before us from Sir Edward Burne-Jones, in which he says: "I was quite unprepared for such fidelity."

By the introduction of the various "processes" by which artists' drawings are nowadays made applicable for reproduction, the days of wood engraving are practically over, and we have to bow to the new light which we had long felt would come; and we need hardly say that, for the reproduction of good pen work, with the new process by line etching, the results are perfect.

Also, when we look at the reproductions of tint drawings by such men as William Small, De Haenen, the Pagets, Caton Woodville, W. L. and C. Wyllie, Edgar Bundy, Jacomb Hood, and many other artists of distinction, by the half-tone process, and when we think (beyond all this fine artistic work) of the vast mass of wonderful illustration given to the public, week by week, of every conceivable class of subject, direct from the camera, in which the draughtsman has no part at all, and this work is generally of singular beauty and truth —we feel that our occupation is gone. In saying this we wish to add that we hail with satisfaction the marvellous results from these many ingenious adaptations of photography, and the consequent wide spread of the art of illustration, which has ever been our greatest delight.

In preparing the contents of this book it would have been impossible to give the many specimens of our work but for the kind and liberal spirit with which our requests were responded to by the various publishers who had entrusted us with their commissions from our very earliest days. Our best thanks are due, in the first instance, to Messrs. Adam & Charles Black, for the loan of two engravings for the "Abbotsford Edition of Scott's Novels," which were amongst our first important works ; the Art Union of London, for a specimen of Kenny Meadows' ; Messrs. Macmillan, for specimens from "The Ingoldsby Legends," "Tennyson's Poems," and "Alice in Wonderland" ; Messrs. Bradbury & Agnew, for selections from Richard Doyle's work ; Messrs. George Routledge & Sons, for specimens from "Gilbert's Shakespeare" and various "Fine Art Books" ; Messrs. Herbert Virtue & Co., for several from Millais' "The Parables of Our Lord" and "Dalziel's Bible Gallery" ; Messrs. Blackwood & Son, for "Lays of the Scottish Cavaliers," by Sir J. Noel Paton ; Messrs. James Nisbet & Co., for "Lays of the Holy Land ; " Messrs. Longman &

Co, for Tenniel's "Lalla Rookh"; Messrs. Smith, Elder & Co., for "Framley Parsonage" and the *Cornhill Magazine;* Mr. James Hogg, for "London Society"; Messrs. D. Appleton & Co., for "Poems by W. Cullen Bryant"; Mr. John Hogg, for "Poems by Robert Buchanan"; Messrs. Chapman & Hall, for many illustrations to the works of Charles Dickens; the Proprietors of the *Graphic,* for "The Sisters," by G. J. Pinwell; and to Messrs. Ward and Lock, for "Dalziel's Arabian Nights" and "Dalziel's Goldsmith."

Mr. Alexander Strahan has our warmest thanks for much help which he kindly gave us in procuring many valuable representative specimens of our work from his various publications.

And yet other thanks are due. Before publishing the letters to be found in the following pages, it was necessary to seek the permission of the writer of each, or the executors of those no longer with us. In every case the response has been so kind and so reminiscent, that the interest and pleasure derived from their receipt will remain till the end with

George and Edward Dalziel

*Hampstead
1901*

LIST OF ILLUSTRATIONS.

Dedicated

IN KIND REMEMBRANCE

OF THE

MANY FRIENDS WHOSE WORKS ADORN THE PAGES

OF THIS BOOK.

THE BROTHERS DALZIEL.

———•———

CHAPTER I.

PARENTAGE—FOUR BROTHERS AND A SISTER. EBENEZER LANDELLS,
THOMAS BEWICK, WILLIAM HARVEY, AND SAMUEL LOVER.

WE were members of a family of twelve children,
and, with one exception, we were born at Wooler,
Northumberland, the youngest having been born at
Newcastle-on-Tyne. Our father spent a great part
of his time in horticultural pursuits, and in middle
life took up art as a profession. He also held a
commission in the Northumberland Militia. His
sons, eight in number, inherited strong artistic
tastes, which they all carried out professionally,
except the youngest, Davison, who applied himself
very successfully to commerce. The eldest, William,
whose art work was chiefly devoted to heraldic and
occasional ornamental decoration for MSS. books,
also painted a little in still-life subjects with remarkable fidelity ; while the second son, Robert,
devoted himself to art, and obtained a fair reputation as a portrait painter. He also studied
landscape painting for some time under Thompson,

of Duddingston, and having practised his art successfully both in Glasgow and Edinburgh, he came
ultimately to London, where he died, having attained
only his thirty-second year. The next brother,
Alexander, was a youth of rare artistic promise,
and, had he lived, must of necessity have made a
great name for himself as a designer and draughtsman in black and white; but early in life, while
living in London, he caught a chill, which terminated in consumption. He, having returned to his
mother's house in Newcastle-on-Tyne, died before
completing his twenty-third year.

The next brother, George, early in 1835,* being
then nineteen, came to London as a pupil to the
late Charles Gray, an engraver on wood, with whom
he remained four years, and on the completion of
his engagement, he commenced operations on his
own account, though continuing on the most friendly
terms with Gray. A few weeks later he was

* With very trifling exceptions there was no railway travelling in
England at that time, and only one steam vessel, the *Hylton Jolliffe*,
sailed between Newcastle and the Metropolis, so that George Dalziel
made the journey in a small trading vessel of some three or four hundred
tons burden. The weather being calm and warm for the season, the
little ship went pleasantly along until it had performed about half the
journey, when, through negligence on the part of the chief mate, who
was in charge at the time, the vessel was allowed to run aground upon a
sand bank when nearly opposite Yarmouth. It was a beautiful sunny
morning, and the ship was quickly surrounded by a great many fishing
boats offering their services to take out part of the cargo, and so lighten
it sufficiently that it might float again when the tide rose. This was done,
and having gone a little further out to sea, the cargo was again put
on board and the ship sailed away to London, where she finally cast
anchor in the Thames nearly opposite the Tower, on a bright, fresh,
Sunday morning, having occupied nearly a whole week in the
journey.

ALEXANDER DALZIEL,

OUR FATHER.

BORN, MAY 22, 1781; DIED, JUNE 30, 1832.

FROM A BUST, MODELLED BY HIS SECOND SON, ROBERT DALZIEL.

———

*"Alexander Dalziel, born at Wooler, in the County of North-
umberland, on the 22nd May, 1781; married at Lamberton, North
Britain, on the 4th day of January, 1805, to Elizabeth Hills, born
at Mornington, North Britain, on the 11th May, 1783."*

—EXTRACT FROM FAMILY BIBLE.

joined by his brother Edward, and from that day
we two have, for a period of over fifty-five years,
worked hand in hand together, as " The Brothers
Dalziel."

In 1852 our brother John became associated with
us.   He was a skilful and highly accomplished
engraver ; but his health, unfortunately, gave way,
and early in 1868 he was compelled to give up all
artistic work and went to reside at Drig, a delightfully picturesque locality, surrounded on the one side
by the Cumberland Lakes and hills, and on the
other by the broad sea, hoping that the fine bracing
air of the North would restore him to health, but
unhappily the change came too late, and he died
in the summer of 1869.

In 1860 our brother Thomas, who had been
educated as a copperplate engraver, joined the
" Brotherhood," and from that time devoted himself
entirely to painting and drawing on wood, contributing much excellent work to the various books
we produced.   Among them may be mentioned
" Dalziel's Arabian Nights," " Dalziel's Bible Gallery "
—of which we will have much to say further on,
and a beautiful edition of " The Pilgrim's Progress,"
as well as many very charming drawings for nearly
all the Fine Art Books created by ourselves, or
produced under our entire supervision.

In the early part of our career, that is to say
during the Forties, we George and Edward, worked
very much in association with Ebenezer Landells,
one of the original projectors and proprietors of

Elizabeth Dalziel,

OUR MUCH-BELOVED MOTHER.

BORN, MAY 11, 1783; DIED, FEBRUARY 4, 1853.

FROM A PICTURE BY HER SECOND SON, ROBERT DALZIEL.
PAINTED ABOUT 1837.

————

*She was one of the brightest, the best, and kindest of women— a true
embodiment of all that is good and just.*

Punch, and from whom (the other original proprietors having resigned their shares in a then unprofitable speculation) Messrs. Bradbury and Evans, the printers, acquired a two-thirds share. Subsequently the entire property passed into their hands. We may here state that while in association with Landells, we engraved the picture, "Foreign Affairs," which was the first drawing contributed to *Punch* by John Leech.

Landells was a man to whom illustrated literature, journalism in particular, owes much. It is an old story, well known at the time, how he parted with his interest in *Punch,* and how he lost the proceeds in the *Illuminated Magazine,* which was edited by Douglas Jerrold. Among his thousand and one journalistic ventures, he was the first to project and produce the *Lady's Newspaper,* but in this, as in other things, he was before his time and failed. He it was who suggested to Herbert Ingram that an artist should be sent to follow the progress of Queen Victoria on her first journey to Scotland; Landells undertook the commission, and it was the success of, and great interest taken in these pictures that had much to do with making the *Illustrated London News.* The Queen was so much pleased, that she bought all Landells' original drawings. He worked very much with Herbert Ingram, and it was through him that we were engaged upon the second number of the *Illustrated London News.* It was for him that we engraved the prospectus block for *Punch,* also the covers for that journal drawn by

GEORGE DALZIEL.

BORN, DECEMBER 1, 1815.

FROM A PICTURE PAINTED BY HIS BROTHER ROBERT.
DATE ABOUT 1841 OR '42.

"Archie" Henning, William Harvey, and John Gilbert, as well as the "H. K. B." drawings every week for "Master Humphrey's Clock." In fact we were largely indebted to him for much sincere help at a time when such help was invaluable, and at his house we had the advantage of forming the friendship of Douglas Jerrold, the Brothers Mayhew, Mark Lemon, and others connected with the foundation of *Punch*.

Landells was a man brimful of ideas and full of energy. One hardly ever met him but that he had some new project which was "certain to be a fortune"—a fortune that never came to him.

His connection with the *Illustrated London News* continued until Herbert Ingram's departure for America, from which place he never returned, having been drowned on Lake Michigan. It is a curious fact that, when Ingram's body was brought home for interment, on the same day that his funeral took place at Boston the remains of Landells were interred at Highgate Cemetery. We were at the ceremonies. Edward attended the one, while George was present at the other.

An interesting anecdote is told of Thomas Bewick in reference to Ebenezer Landells. When it was proposed to place him as a pupil with that eminent wood engraver, the father of the lad said, "Well, Mr. Bewick, I hope you will make my son a clever fellow." "Mr. Landells," replied the veteran, "I'll do my best to teach him what I know, but if God Almighty hasn't put brains into your son's head, it's impossible for me to put them there!"

EDWARD DALZIEL.

BORN, DECEMBER 5, 1817.

FROM A PICTURE PAINTED BY HIS BROTHER ROBERT.
DATE ABOUT 1841 OR '42.

This anecdote was told us by Landells himself, in illustration of a principle he was discussing, that unless a lad has a real, genuine love for the art he is studying, no teaching in the world will ever make him a skilful worker. His father not being able to arrange terms with Bewick, Landells did not remain long with him, but served his apprenticeship with Isaac Nicholson (an old pupil of Bewick's, who had opened an office on the opposite side of the way to his old master, in St. Nicholas' Churchyard, New-castle-on-Tyne), with whom Charles Gray was also a pupil. And it was through those two young men coming to our Father to "learn to draw" that our brother Alexander became a pupil of Nicholson's, with whom he served a seven years' apprenticeship, and proved himself a very skilful draughtsman and engraver. Hence our somewhat close connection with the school of Thomas Bewick.

Landells was a man of slightly excitable temperament, and, as a rule, very demonstrative. One morning he called upon his old pupil, Edmund Evans, who was then commencing colour printing works in Racquet Court, saying "he was off to the Derby, and, as the morning looked rather doubtful, would he lend him an umbrella?" This Evans most willingly did, giving the best he had, almost a new one. Landells faithfully returned it the next morning, but the ferrule had disappeared, and the stick was battered down close to the silk. Landells had evidently been through some exciting scenes, and in expressing his high appreciation of the events Evans' umbrella had come sadly to grief.

When Landells got a little vexed or worried by
anyone, which in his very much varied life he not
unfrequently did, his invariable remark was, "Well,
stop till I see him again and I'll give him a piece
of my mind."

JOHN DALZIEL.

BORN, JANUARY 1, 1822; DIED, MAY 21, 1869.

FROM A PHOTOGRAPH

During the time that "ructions" were on with
his co-partners in *Punch*, he met Douglas Jerrold in
Fleet Street and complained bitterly, winding up with,
"There, I've just been to see them and have given

them a bit of my mind." "Ah," said Jerrold, "I'm afraid they would not gain much by that, Landells."

His eldest son, Robert Landells, also an artist of considerable ability in black and white work, acted for many years as Art War Correspondent to the *Illustrated London News,* and, in that capacity, went through a great part of the Franco Prussian Campaign.

The years of our boyhood having been spent in Newcastle-on-Tyne, we have constantly been identified as being natives of the Tyneside, and so became much associated with several artists of ability who hailed from that part of the kingdom. Among the foremost of those we would mention William Harvey, the justly celebrated artist and book illustrator, who was himself a favourite pupil of Thomas Bewick, and during his apprenticeship designed and engraved several of the smaller tailpieces to the "Fables," "Natural History," and other works published by his famous master.

William Harvey was born at Newcastle-on-Tyne, July 13th, 1796, and died at Richmond, Surrey, January 18th, 1866. He was apprenticed to Thomas Bewick, 1810, and the high esteem in which he was held by his master is shown in the letter here quoted.

"GATESHEAD, *January 1st, 1815.*

"DEAR WILLIAM,—I sent you last night, 'The History of British Birds,' which I beg your acceptance of as a New Year's gift and also as a token of my respect. Don't trouble yourself about thanking me for them ; but, instead of doing so, let those books put you in mind of the duties you have to perform through life. Look at them (as long as they last) on every New Year's day, and at the same time resolve, with the help of the All-wise but unknowable God, to conduct yourself on every occasion as becomes a good man. Be a good son, a good brother, and (when the time comes)

THOMAS DALZIEL.

BORN, MAY 9, 1823.

FROM A PHOTOGRAPH.

a good husband, a good father, and a good member of Society. Peace of mind will then follow you like a shadow; and when your mind grows rich in integrity, you will fear the frowns of no man, and only smile at the plots and conspiracies which it is probable will be laid against you by envy, hatred, and malice.

"THOMAS BEWICK.

"To William Harvey, Junr.,
        " Westgate."

Two years later, 1817, when he had completed his apprenticeship, he went to London, where he studied drawing and painting under Benjamin Haydon, and anatomy with Sir Charles Bell, where he had, as fellow students, amongst others, Charles Lock Eastlake, the P.R.A., George Lance, the fruit painter, and Sir Edwin Landseer. He soon became a most distinguished draughtsman and illustrator of books, his fame rising rapidly. For many years he stood prominently in the front of all others. Amongst his earliest works were " Henderson's Book on Wines," for which he not only made the drawings but engraved them all himself. It is further interesting as being the first work that bore his name. His great ability both as draughtsman and engraver is shown in the reproduction of an elaborate work from Benjamin Haydon's picture of " Dentatus "—which even in these advanced days must be held as a remarkable example of wood engraving, being, strictly speaking, a marvellous imitation of a copperplate, done in the grand line manner. Haydon no doubt induced Harvey to undertake this work to satisfy his own vanity, for he was not a man " who cared for others."

About this time he gave up engraving altogether and devoted himself entirely to drawing on wood.

William Harvey was a great and highly-gifted artist, a true man, a friend and counsellor to us from the time of our earliest efforts to the day of his death. He was a fine conversationalist, brimful of anecdotes, chiefly concerning a notable group of artists, authors, and men of law, many of whom had gone, and others who were then passing away. As an illustrator he held the town for many years, and in connection with Charles Knight did much to popularise black and white work; but even in his own time what changes took place! He said that

in his early days if merely a frontispiece were wanted for a book, John Murray would invite him and John Thomson, the engraver, to dinner at Albemarle Street, that they might discuss the subject fully before beginning the work.

In his more important works Harvey always tried to push forward one or more young and unknown engravers of promise—in fact he was the young man's friend.

Of course he had many imitators ; coming men begin by imitating the manner of the successful men who have gone before. He used to say, " The young man jumps on the shoulders of the old man, looks over his head, and consequently sees much farther along the road." Strong examples of this are shown in the early works of Sir John Gilbert, which alternated in likeness to William Harvey, Kenny Meadows, and George Cruikshank ; but in a later stage took on much from the great German artist, Menzel.

The following are a few instances in illustration of young men building up their style by studying the old professors in their art, which we call to mind as occurring in our own experience :

William Harvey felt complimented by John Gilbert gleaning from his works ; while George Cruikshank was highly indignant with Gilbert for what he called " cribbing his brains," and threatened to go down to Blackheath and " thrash the fellow." Gilbert, on being told this, only laughed, and said, " I don't think he knows what sort of man I am."

J. Prior, the father of Melton Prior, assisted William Harvey very frequently ; and after acquiring a fair style of imitation, did a good deal of work on his own account, which sometimes bore too strong a resemblance to the master. He would say to Harvey, " I know you don't mind." He was right ; good-natured Harvey did not mind if Prior got any advantage by it. But, like other men, Prior ultimately acquired a style of his own, and did much good service in the early days of the *Illustrated London News*, to which journal his son Melton has long been a valuable power as War Correspondent.

The early drawings of that great art genius, Fred Walker, A.R.A., R.W.S., have a strong family resemblance to those of Sir John Gilbert. J. W. North's early drawings reminded one vividly of Birket Foster, while Birket Foster's style was un-doubtedly built upon Thomas Creswick, R.A.—and so on, and so on.

Our connection with Harvey was so close, not only as regards work, but socially, that we can say he was in every sense one of "Nature's best"; lovable to a degree,—and would far more than stand the test of the guiding-lines laid down by his master in the letter printed on page 12.

Among William Harvey's chief works mention must be made of the charmingly fanciful designs for Lane's "Arabian Nights," "Northcoat's Fables," "The Tower Menagerie," several of the books in "The Abbotsford Edition" of Sir Walter Scott's novels, and many smaller books, notably "The Children in the Wood," and "The Blind Beggar's Daughter of Bethnal Green"; also an extremely beautiful frontis-piece, as well as other illustrations, to each of the plays in Charles Knight's Edition of Shakespeare's Works. Subsequently he illustrated for us an edition of "The Pilgrim's Progress," in which he displayed all his tasteful fancy in decorating its pages. This book was published by David Bogue. From 1839 to the time of his death, William Harvey entrusted

B

many of his drawings to our care, as well as in later years constantly working for the various books produced under our superintendence.

On the death of William Harvey, it was proposed that a monument should be erected over his grave in Richmond cemetery, and in seeking subscriptions for that purpose, among others, Samuel Lover, the famous Irish song-writer, composer and artist, was asked to assist and co-operate with a few friends in carrying out the object, when in reply he wrote :

"I wish instead of a few friends that many were engaged for what is proposed, for then this monument might be much more worthy the memory of so good an artist and so good a man.   As to the extent, you may rely on me for help . . . In sincere esteem for my much esteemed friend, I think few can exceed me, but my exchequer is rather limited.   Could I convert my heart into a bank, and make its wishes into bank notes, I would build a monument out of my own purse to one so worthy of esteem and every kind remembrance.

"Truly,

"SAMUEL LOVER."

Is not this just the letter we might expect from the warm-hearted Irishman and true poet who could write the following beautiful lines ?

" I'll seek a four-leaved shamrock in all the fairy dells,
And if I find the charmed leaves, oh, how I'll weave my spells !
I would not waste my magic might on diamond, pearl or gold,
For treasure tires the weary sense—such triumph is but cold.
But I would play the enchanter's part in casting bliss around,
And not a tear or aching heart should in the world be found."

The monument was erected, as suggested, in the cemetery at Richmond, Surrey, as well as a brass tablet in St. Nicholas' Cathedral, Newcastle-on-Tyne, both from designs by John R. Clayton.

Having furnished several illustrations to a book of Irish songs edited by Samuel Lover, and published by John Maxwell, husband of Miss Braddon, we received several kind letters of commendation and thanks for the care bestowed in getting up the work. Among others we may quote the following :

"*November 13th, 1857.*

"I hope you will excuse me for not having sooner acknowledged your enclosure of your engraving of Gratton's Head, which is quite admirable, and for which I truly thank you."

Again, in writing of a drawing to illustrate the "Four-leaved Shamrock," which we had submitted for his approval, he says :

"I think your quadruple design most excellent. If that be carried out (as I have no doubt it will) with the care and spirit of the drawing on the wood, it will make a charming illustration. . . . I suggest that you place the initial letter 'I' encircled with the charmed leaves in the corner, to commence the first line of the song. I am glad for your own sake, as well as for the credit of the book, you have made the second illustration, as I am convinced it will do you much credit. For myself, pray accept my many thanks.

"My dear Sirs,

"Yours very truly,

"Samuel Lover."

During all our operations from the year 1851, we were fortunate enough to have the loyal and skilful help of our sister Margaret, who warmly entered into all our plans and worked very constantly upon the most highly finished engravings we

produced. As much of the work we were engaged
upon was intended for periodical publications, it
may readily be supposed that there was, at times,
great pressure to meet the requirements of the

MARGARET DALZIEL.

BORN, NOVEMBER 3, 1819; DIED, JULY 12, 1894.

FROM A PHOTOGRAPH.

———

She was the essence of kindness and generosity, a sister-mother to
us all, and "Aunt Meg" to everybody.

printer ; on such occasions we could always be
certain of her ever ready help, grudging neither
time nor labour to render every assistance in her
power. In all respects she was one of the most

devoted, kind-hearted and sympathetic women that
ever lived, and her great excellence of character, we
have every reason to believe, was fully appreciated
by all those who had the privilege of her acquaintance or friendship.

THE EARL OF LEICESTER'S LEVEE.
FROM THE ABBOTSFORD EDITION OF "KENNILWORTH.
BY WILLIAM HARVEY.

By permission of Messrs. Adam & Charles Black.

CHAPTER II.

VERY early in our career we were, through our
friend William Harvey, introduced to Charles Knight,
the eminent publisher who did so much as a pioneer
in introducing cheap and good literature to the
people, as his " Penny Magazine," " Penny Cyclo-
pædia," " Charles Knight's History of England," and
many other kindred works bear ample evidence.
And not only in literature but in art as well he
took a bold and leading part: see his elaborately
illustrated edition of Shakespeare's Works, the Bible,
" The Land we Live in," and many highly interesting and instructive books. Perhaps the most
beautiful of all was the illustrated edition of Lane's
" Arabian Nights' Entertainments," a book which
must always hold a foremost place among the most
tastefully decorated volumes this country has produced.

It was only in association with Landells and
Charles Gray that we were at all connected with
this work, not having, at that time, any personal
transaction with Mr. Knight, though we subsequently
did a great deal of work for him, notably in his
" Shakespeare" and " The Land we Live in."

Mr. Ramsay, Mr. Knight's sub-editor and literary

manager, used to tell a curious story about one of
the literary contributors to these volumes, whose
name, for obvious reasons, we will withhold.

In this gentleman's early connection with Mr.
Knight, he called and had a serious conversation
with Ramsay, confessing his uncontrollable weak-
ness for strong drink, and that his only safeguard
was an empty pocket. He therefore begged of
Ramsay never, under any circumstances, to advance
him one penny upon his work, no matter how hard
he might plead, or what story he might tell in
urging the necessity for an advance of cash. Ramsay
was to be firm and refuse to listen to him, and on
no account to let him have money, and that all payment for work was to be forwarded to his wife.
Ramsay promised faithful observance, and so matters
went smoothly on for a considerable time. But one
day M. N. came with a sad, doleful face, begging
for an advance of ten pounds. Ramsay positively
declined, reminding him of their compact.

"Yes, yes, that's all right, old fellow," he answered; "but this business is quite away from
everything else. I don't forget the injunction I
laid upon you, but this is altogether different; it is
a case of the most urgent necessity." Then he went
on and told a sad, touching tale of his boy having
died suddenly, and the shock having brought on a
serious illness with his wife, while, unfortunately, he
was totally without funds to meet the unexpected
demands upon his purse, or procure a nurse to
attend upon her, as well as the comforts that were
absolutely necessary under the circumstances.

For a time Ramsay stood firmly out, always reminding M. N. of his own proposition, but the man was so impressively urgent, appealing again and again on the score of his wife's critical condition, that at last Ramsay's scruples gave way, and M. N., lavish in his thanks, left the office with the ten pounds in his pocket.

It is, perhaps, needless to say that M. N. was not seen in Fleet Street for many days, and when he did turn up, shaky and dilapidated in appearance, it was only to load Ramsay with the most crushing abuse for having broken faith with him, and when Ramsay tried to shelter himself under the pathetic tale he had told about his sick wife and dead son, he only replied :

" D—— the sick wife and dead son ! Why didn't you stick to your promise ? I told you distinctly that it was possible I might come with some trumped-up story of urgent necessity, and a lot of such rubbish, and now see what a hole you have let me into. My son is perfectly well, and as healthy a lad as ever lived, and as for my wife, well, she was never better in her life, and is only suffering from the misery brought about by your unaccountably bad behaviour to me. I tell you, Ramsay, you are a traitor and a false friend, who has used me shamefully—shamefully ! "

With these words M. N. left the office, but returned within half an hour seeking condonation, begging that Ramsay would overlook the foolish words he had used in a moment of unjustifiable irritation, and further show his good feeling by

MACKAY, AS THE BAILIE NICOL JARVIE.

FROM THE ABBOTSFORD EDITION OF "ROB ROY."

FROM A PAINTING BY SIR WILLIAM ALLAN, R.A., P.R.S.A.

By permission of Messrs. Adam & Charles Black.

advancing him a trifle—say, a sovereign? No?
Well, then, let it be five shillings? Still no! Ramsay
was obdurate, and M. N., muttering, "Cruel man!
Cruel, cruel man!" went away.

In the year 1842 or 1843, through the kindness
of the late Clarkson Stanfield, R.A., we were introduced to Mr. William Dicks, who officiated as

art agent for Mr. Cadell, the Edinburgh publisher,
then issuing a very elaborately illustrated edition of
the Waverley Novels, which he named " The Abbotsford Edition," and employing on the work many
of the very first artists of the day, both English and
Scotch. We were entrusted to engrave a large
number of the drawings. Among the first of these
was a wonderfully life-like portrait of the Scotch
actor, Mackay, in the character of " Bailie Nicol
Jarvie," painted by Sir William Allan, R.A. and
P.R.S.A.* The engraving of this portrait gave
such entire satisfaction both to Mr. Cadell and
Mr. Dicks that we were constantly employed upon
the undertaking until its completion.

Among the artists whose drawings we had to
engrave during the progress of this edition of the
great " Wizard of the North's" novels, we may
especially mention William Harvey, Clarkston Stanfield, R.A., Sir J. Noel Paton, P.R.S.A., John Franklin,
Edward H. Corbould, Sir David Wilkie, R.A.,
Alexander Christie, and Robert McIan.

Through the friendship that sprung up with
several of these gentlemen, and our connection with
the Institute of the Fine Arts,† we became acquainted
with many of the young artists who were introducing
a new and more realistic feeling into the black and
white work of the day. Among them were John
Tenniel, at that time just returned from his studies

---

* It is stated that Sir Walter Scott was so delightfully charmed with
Mackay's acting in this character that he declared "until he saw him act
he had no idea of the extraordinary character he had drawn."

† An Institution long since defunct.

in Germany, and strongly impressed with German Art, and what was termed "The Shaded Outline School"; Alfred Elmore, R.A.; Fred Pickersgill,

CHILDREN IN THE WOOD. BY JOHN FRANKLIN.

FROM CUNDALL'S SERIES OF CHILDREN'S BOOKS.

R.A.; F. W. Topham; Edward Duncan; George Dodgson; John Absolon; all, except the Royal Academicians, members of the Old Water Colour

Society, and the New—now called the Royal
Institute of Water Colour Painters—besides many
others who have since risen to great eminence in
their profession.

John Absolon being then engaged on a set of
illustrations to Collins' Poetical Works, to be published by David Bogue, he placed many of the
drawings in our hands to engrave, which was the
commencement of a long and intimate friendship—
not only with the artist, for it also opened up a
connection with Bogue which enabled us to produce
some very creditable works together.

Early in 1851 John Franklin, many of whose illustrations to " The Abbotsford Scott " and the " British
Ballads " we had engraved, placed in our hands some
drawings he was making to illustrate a series of Fairy
Tales, edited by Sir Henry Cole, then known to the
literary world as " Felix Summerly," to be published
by Mr. Joseph Cundall of Bond Street, who was an
enlightened publisher with strong artistic taste, his
great idea being a desire to raise the character of
children's picture books.   This was about the time
that Van Voorst published " The Vicar of Wakefield,"
with Mulready's illustrations ; one of the first high-
class books of the period, which was so highly
thought of that Mulready said he had commissions
offered to him for pictures from these designs
sufficient to keep him at work for the remainder of
his life.   It was at this time that Cundall induced
Mulready to make a set of drawings for a child's
primer : and very beautiful they are.

This series of Fairy Tales was continued, with

pictures by Frederick Taylor, P.R.W.S., H. C. Horsley, R.A., and other artists of high repute.

Our connection with these two London publishing houses, added to the work we were doing for Mr. Cadell of Edinburgh, tended considerably to increase our responsibilities.   And this may be the

SLEEPING CHILD AND LAMB.   BY WILLIAM MULREADY, R.A.

FROM A BOOK OF POEMS BY THE REV. T. J. JUDKIN.

most convenient place to state that it was at Mr. Cundall's we were first introduced to Mr. George Routledge, who had called for the express purpose of asking Mr. Cundall to recommend a "good man" to engrave a small drawing on wood, a portrait of Sir Robert Peel, which he then had in his pocket.

The commission was entrusted to us, and thus commenced a connection and a friendship which continued
with unabated confidence and harmony for a period
extending over forty years.

George Routledge, a strong-minded, clear-headed
man of business, in his early days used to go per-
sonally to the larger north country towns, and get
orders from the booksellers. His capacity in this
branch was said to be something marvellous. An
old Quaker bookseller, of Darlington, told us that
Routledge never said, " Will thee buy this book?"
but that it always was with him, " Thee must take
it"; and as his wares were always good, the results
were said to be many times beyond those of any
other man " on the road." In the publishing business,
he, in combination with his partners, William and
Frederick Warne—both clever, energetic men,—made
a force which developed their vast business so rapidly
that Henry G. Bohn, the big publisher of that
day, felt so jealous of their great success, that he
used to say, " Well, it has taken three strong men
to do it." After having produced sets of pictures
by various artists, to many sorts of books, the most
important of which was a small octavo of Longfellow's Poems, with illustrations by John Gilbert,
they invited our co-operation, assistance, and direction
in such matters, and it was then determined to do
another edition of the same poems, more extensively
illustrated by the same artist. They agreed to give
us one thousand pounds for the pictures, which was
to include Gilbert's charges as well as our own. The
book proved a great success from every point of

view, and to this day holds its own as one of the most beautiful examples of Sir John Gilbert's work as an illustrator. After the first edition many other poems were added, including " Miles Standish," all having Gilbert's illustrations to them.*

The book when first completed created a sensation. We remember asking Routledge what he thought of it. He was a pure business man. His reply was:

"We will wait and see what the trade has to say about it first—see whether they will subscribe

---

* The following lines, which were largely quoted by the American Press, were written on the occasion of Canon Prothero unveiling a bust of Henry Wadsworth Longfellow, in Westminster Abbey, March 1st, 1884:

There is no place in all the great wide world,
 Where Anglo-Saxon is the spoken tongue,
Or where the British flag streams out unfurled,
 Where patriotic song or ballad's sung,—
But there is heard in kindly company
 With Burns and Hood, with Dibdin, Goldsmith, Moore,
The name of him from far across the sea
 Who sang the noble song, Excelsior.

He touched the heart with sweet and silvery rhyme,—
 He thrilled us with the pathos of his song,—
He showed us wild men in the olden time,
 And painted suff'ring under cruel wrong.
Yet ever in the light of truest love
 He swept with tender touch the sacred lyre ;
And as he sang he caught, as from above,
 A blaze of holy, pure, poetic fire.

He sang of changing seasons warm and bright,
 He sang of times that were all cold and grey ;
He sang of Flowers and of the darkening night,
 Of Angel footsteps, and of Rainy day ;—

largely, and then I will tell you what I think about it."

Edmondson, the binder, was so in love with his part of the work that, holding the volume in his hands, he said, " It is a beautiful book ! a very beautiful book !" then added, in a slightly condescending tone, " And a good book inside, too."

William Warne dying rather early in life, Frederick Warne, his younger brother, separated from the Routledges, after the sons of George entered

---

Of Blacksmith as he by the anvil stood,
 The Skipper and his daughter drowned at sea,
The Maiden stepping into womanhood,
 And then God's Acre, with its mystery.

E'en as he sang, so lived he in his day,
 Aye striving for some good deed to be done,—
To show some thing of beauty by the way,
 And tell how fame and honour might be won.
" His life was beautiful," * so sang his friend,
 With constant charity of heart and hand ;
This one more chaplet with his name we blend,—
 " He was an honour to his native land." *

To-day we lay a humble tribute bare,
 'Tis but a block of marble, in the place,
On which a human hand, with cunning rare,
 Has deftly carved the sweetness of his face.
There in the Abbey, where our poets lie,
 Where many a noble pageant we have seen,
Stands now this bust—where all the world may hie—
 Of him who told us of Evangeline.

                                   GEORGE DALZIEL.

---

* These words were used by the American Ambassador, who was present and spoke on the occasion.

EVANGELINE.

FROM THE POETICAL WORKS OF LONGFELLOW.

ILLUSTRATED BY SIR JOHN GILBERT, R.A., P.R.W.S.

By permission of Messrs. George Routledge & Sons.

the firm, and built up a large publishing house of
his own. We were on the very best of terms
with all of them, and continued to work for both
houses for many, many years.

C

Frederick Warne, a really clever, many-sided man, has now retired, but his three sons—all men worthy of their father—continue to conduct their large business on the old lines.

Of the many illustrated books which it has been our lot to superintend and issue to the world, there are two for which we are to a great extent exclusively responsible : these are " The Spirit of Praise," a collection of hymns, and " Golden Thoughts from Golden Fountains," a collection of such literary extracts from favourite authors as the title of the book will fully explain—one of us having spent much of his leisure hours in collecting and arranging their contents. The first of these volumes was originally published in the usual quarto form, with decorative borders and initial letters, printed in gold and colours, and subsequently much enlarged by the addition of many hymns as an octavo volume. The other, " Golden Thoughts," was in its main lines uniform with the first edition of " The Spirit of Praise." In both of these books are many of our own contributions, both in pen and pencil, in addition to several very fine examples of A. B. Houghton.

" The Abbotsford Edition " of the Waverley Novels did not prove a marked financial success, and when the property was acquired by Messrs. Adam and Charles Black, Edward H. Corbould, R.I., was commissioned to do a large number of illustrations for their new edition of these books, nearly all of which were entrusted to us to engrave.

In the early part of Queen Victoria's reign Corbould held a high position as a painter in

water colour, and was one of the original members
of the " Royal Institute of Water Colour Painters"
—then called the " New Water Colour Society "
—and so highly was his artistic ability appreciated
by the Prince Consort that he was selected as
art tutor to the Royal children. Perhaps no better
selection could at that time have been made ; for,
though somewhat severe in style, he was a good
draughtsman, painstaking, and of a kindly, genial
disposition. He was ever full of amusing anecdotes
of the sayings and doings of the Queen, Prince
Albert, and his pupils.

Corbould did not appear to think it possible
for any of those young people to commit a fault.
In his eyes they were all sweetness and the
perfection of goodness, " being," as he said, " without
the least appearance of affectation." When asked
if any of the young Princes or Princesses were
clever, he invariably evaded a direct answer by
saying :

" Er—well, you see, the Princess Royal makes
up for the shortcomings of all the others, she is
so very clever. Er—er—they are all clever and
very nice."

During Corbould's connection with the Royal
Family, on one occasion he wrote to us saying
the Prince of Wales had got a scrap-book, and
he was commissioned by the Prince to say how
pleased he would be if we would give him some
proofs of our engravings to put into it. We
sent a large parcel, and in return Corbould wrote
that the Prince was delighted with our contribu-

tion and wished him to express his " Warmest
thanks to Messrs. Dalziel for their great kindness
and liberality."

> " *26 July, 1863,*
> " 21 RUTLAND GATE,
> " HYDE PARK.

" DEAR SIRS,—I have received the impression, as well as my
own, as also the proof for the Prince of Wales. I shall be at
Osborne either on Thursday or Friday next, and I will give it
to him. That which you engraved for the 'Keepsake, 1854,' is
very beautiful, and so I shall keep the proof. Mr. Heath will
be quite content and so shall I. You can tell him that I
require nothing done to it. I thank you for the proof, but
where are those from Spencer ? *

> " Yours very truly,
> " EDWARD HENRY CORBOULD."

During the early part of our career we became
associated with Mr. Samuel Carter Hall, who was
originator, editor and at that time proprietor of the
Art Journal, and in a somewhat desultory fashion
did a considerable amount of work together. Among
other matters, we engraved many of the illustrations
for " A Book of British Ballads," which was edited
by Hall and published by Messrs. How and Parsons
of Fleet Street. The drawings by Sir J. Noel
Paton, P.R.S.A., John Franklin, W. B. Scott, E. H.
Corbould, Henry Warren, and other artists, passed
through our hands. When the great International
Exhibition of 1851 was in preparation, and during
the time it was open to the public, Hall published
a series of profusely illustrated supplements to the

---

* Corbould had made a set of eight illustrations to Spencer's
" Fairy Queen " for us.

Art Journal, showing the various classes of objects exhibited. On this work we were very liberally employed. These supplements were subsequently put together and published in one large, handsome quarto volume as an Illustrated Catalogue of that great and important Exhibition.

Many other catalogues, official and non-official, were published of the Exhibition, which contained a marvellous amount of every conceivable class of handicraft and ingenious device, but certainly, for comprehensive completeness, none of them at all approached the very beautiful volume which Mr. Hall gave to the world.

When we had finished our portion of the engravings, he was so grateful for the help we had given that he volunteered the promise that no other wood engravers should ever be employed upon his works. But perhaps it is only characteristic of the man to say that this promise was never carried out.

As already stated, we engraved a very large number of drawings for Mr. Hall with undeviating approval, and we were much gratified by the following passage in a letter addressed to him by E. M. Ward, the Royal Academician, on our submitting a proof of an engraving we had executed :

"The cut is admirable in every way. I have nearly finished the drawing of 'The Royal Family of France,' and will send it immediately it is done. I hope you will have the 'Royal Family' done by Dalziels', as you said it should be ; they would manage the faces much better than——

"Yours ever truly,

"E. M. WARD."

Almost as a matter of course we became associated with Kenny Meadows, a clever, erratic genius,
and an artist of great ability. He had a wonderful and strangely fanciful imagination, and perhaps
will be best known in time to come by his
"Illustrated Shakespeare" and his " Heads of the
People"; there is one other work which is not likely
to be forgotten, "A Head of 'Old Father Christmas,'" which did good service for a Christmas
number of the *Illustrated London News*. He
was intimately connected with Orrin Smith, the
distinguished wood engraver; their earliest work
being character sketches and heads of the people
done for *Bell's Life in London*, which was somewhat a pioneer in illustrated journalism. Meadows
at that time was generally known as "Iron Jack,"
from the fact of his robust health, which he
attributed entirely to a simple style of living in
his early life, much of which was spent in a
lighthouse, where, he declared, they never had
enough to eat. He said, "I used to devour my
food like a ravening wolf."

No amount of alcohol ever appeared to hurt
him, and to those who suffered from excess of
indulgence he attributed it entirely to over-eating in
their early days, before the constitution was fairly
and properly formed.

We were so closely connected with him that
when he was first asked to work for *Punch*, he
stipulated that we should have all his drawings to
engrave. This arrangement did not last long, for
he was of a very uncertain nature, and changeable

"*Or sweetest Shakespeare, Fancy's child,*
Warble his native wood-notes wild."

"L'Allegro" and "Il Penseroso."—MILTON.

BY KENNY MEADOWS.

in his moods. His friendship was not of the kind that would stand much, if any, strain, and after he had "imbibed" a little, he not infrequently became "nasty." Once at a public dinner, on the name of *Punch* being mentioned, he started from his chair, saying, "Gentlemen, I am *Punch!*" which really was more than insulting to several *Punch* men who were present.

At one of the early *Illustrated News* dinners, Herbert Ingram, speaking of the great success of the journal, said, "And, gentlemen, we all share in the credit of producing this wonderful paper." Meadows was immediately on his legs, saying, "Yes, but have we all shared and shared alike in the recompense?" "Yes, Mr. Meadows," said Ingram, "we have all shared alike, according to what we put into the venture."

While Meadows worked for the *Illustrated London News* we engraved many of his drawings and saw much of Herbert Ingram and his partners, Nathaniel Cook and William Little. Ingram was the founder and principal proprietor of the paper; a man of strong character, self-willed, but both generous and just. We were in the habit of suggesting and pro-curing subjects for them.

We had induced Richard Doyle to make twelve drawings of the months for the *Illustrated London Almanack*. Nathaniel Cook disputed our charge, but we stood out. Ingram sat quiet whilst the talk went on. At last he said, "Have Messrs. Dalziel done the work well?" "Oh! there is no dispute about that; the work is well done." "Then," said

Ingram, "pay the money and let there be no dispute about it."

That is a single, but a true, illustration of the
sort of man Herbert Ingram was.

Meadows used to say that Nature put him out,
and so it did. Looking at his raised hand with
pointed finger, he would say, "I cannot see a hand
as I would draw it."

The first time Meadows met John Leech after
he began to draw on *Punch*, he raved about the
drawings, said Leech was the greatest man who
had ever drawn on wood, that he, Meadows, ought
to retire from art altogether and seek some other
occupation, that his light was out, and much more
to the same purpose. But as the bottle went
round, the feeling gradually changed, and it ended
in Meadows praising his own work and telling
Leech that he must alter his style altogether if he
ever hoped to take a position as an artist—that
his work was mere common-place drivel, and that
he must put imagination into his work "such as I
do in mine, sir."

But judged by his time, Meadows was a very
clever man with much quaint fancy. Many of his
initials are singularly pretty, and his "Shakespeare"
will always have a place in the history of black
and white work.

In Kenny Meadows' days, the artist in black
and white had not thought of the advantages of
drawing from the living model; neither William
Harvey nor Sir John Gilbert ever drew from Nature,
and George Thomas was one of the first, if not

indeed the very first, to draw on wood direct from life. This was about the early part of the Crimean War, and his subjects were chiefly of sailors and their doings, and very clever they were. It created something of a sensation at the time, for the idea of an illustration being drawn from the life had not before been heard of except in special cases. No doubt Mulready had life models for his "Vicar of Wakefield" drawings, and later on Millais never drew without the life, nor did any of the pre-Raphaelite School, but this was the gradual and natural development of a new method, and innumerable drawings by the younger artists which passed through our hands were all drawn direct on wood from the life.

After spending much time and labour in experimenting, as well as spoiling a great many blocks, we succeeded in getting fairly good photographs for the engraver's purpose on other pieces of wood, and so the valuable original drawings were preserved. This success was obtained about the beginning, though not at the very beginning, of our operation on the Bible illustrations. Then followed, as a matter of course, the constant practice of making drawings upon paper which were photographed on wood. By this means nearly all the exquisite drawings in black and white made by Leighton, Poynter, Houghton, and many other of the artists who worked in association with us have been preserved, and now adorn some of the public permanent galleries.

Among the early drawings by John Leech that passed through our hands were those he made for

A BALL-ROOM. BY FREDERICK WALKER, A.R.A., R.W.S.
FROM "LONDON SOCIETY."

By permission of Mr. James Hogg.

Thackeray's "Irish Sketch Book," which were probably copied from Thackeray's own pencil work, for
he was not above having help on his drawings,
the result not always being such as he expected.
One day he said to Joseph Swain, "Why don't you
engrave my drawings to come out like John Gilbert's
—his work always looks so strong and mine so weak
and scratchy?" Swain tried other helping hands,
but seldom with satisfactory results. It was in this
way that Fred Walker's connection with Thackeray
began, Swain having induced him to work on the
author's drawings, which he did on one or two,
but very soon declined to go on with them.
Walker asked that he might make original drawings
direct from the story in his own manner, to which
Thackeray agreed; and the result was a fine set of
drawings for "Philip" and for other stories, as well
as a close friendship between author and artist, only
broken by the death of the great novelist.

We engraved many of Leech's drawings, notably
the first he did for *Punch*—"Foreign Affairs" (as
before mentioned). It was a full page, and had to
be worked at from the moment it came into our
hands till it was given to the printer.

John Leech, speaking of Frith's picture of "The
Derby Day," could not understand how it was that
Frith, in this carefully thought out and elaborate
work, had missed one of the most notable facts at
such places—inasmuch as he had not depicted anyone of the crowd smoking a pipe or cigar.

The vain, versatile George Cruikshank believed
himself another "Admirable Crichton." He really

A LAY OF ST. DUNSTAN. BY GEORGE CRUIKSHANK.

FROM THE "INGOLDSBY LEGENDS."

By permission of Messrs. Macmillan & Co.

thought he could do anything, and that most of
his time having been spent as an illustrator was the
result of circumstance and not of choice. He was
impressionable in the highest degree, and depending
on the subject under notice, immediately realised
and expressed his ideas of what "should be done,

and what he would have done if things had favoured him for a career in that direction." Once, the question being of a naval character, he said, "It was by the merest chance that I did not go into the Navy; and with my knowledge of such matters, no doubt I would have been a Rear-Admiral." He was great, also, on the Army, and no doubt felt that had circumstances drifted him in that direction, he would have become another Duke of Wellington. No man ever had greater faith in self than the clever, excitable George Cruikshank.

On the occasion of his exhibiting a small oil picture at the British Institution, called "The Dropped Penny," the fact that it was purchased by Prince Albert no doubt called extra special attention to it, to the extent that it might have been sold many times over. One gentleman was most anxious to have it; or, if this was impossible, would he make a replica? This George declined to do, but undertook a commission, only on the understanding that choice of subject and of size were to be left to him. This was readily agreed to. "The Dropped Penny" was a little thing about 18 by 24 inches. It was a comic picture—two urchins in church, one of whom having dropped a penny on the stone floor is about to pick it up, but they are observed by the Beadle.

When the new work was completed, the gentleman was invited to see it. He found, to his amazement, a picture 16 feet by 20 feet; subject, "The Raising of Lazarus."

THE LORD OF TOULOUSE.   BY SIR JOHN TENNIEL.
FROM THE "INGOLDSBY LEGENDS."

George always thought his true forte was the Grand Historical, and with much cause, when we think of his wonderful illustrations to Harrison Ainsworth's "Tower of London," "Windsor Castle," and other romantic histories.

In the illustrated edition of the "Ingoldsby Legends," published by Messrs. R. Bentley & Son, we had the good fortune to engrave nearly all the drawings contributed by John Tenniel and George Cruikshank.   During the progress of the

work we saw much of the latter gentleman, who
was an exceedingly entertaining companion, being
always ready with some anecdotes or reminiscences
of his experience.   Amongst his many grievances
(and George Cruikshank's stock was an assorted
one) he complained bitterly of the treatment he had
received at the hands of Charles Dickens, with
reference to the authorship of "Oliver Twist."
Cruikshank maintained "that he had not only
suggested the subject to Dickens, but that he had
also given him the entire plot, sketched the characters, arranged all the incidents, and, in fact,
constructed the entire story; so much so, indeed,
that the book was, to all intents and purposes,
HIS; for all that Dickens had to do with it was
TO WRITE IT OUT, and any man who could hold a
pen might have done it better"; concluding with,
"I am only sorry now I didn't do it myself."
Those were the old man's identical words, as
spoken to us.

On one of his visits he related the following
interesting circumstances in connection with his
famous publication of "The Bottle." *   This was a
series of pictures, the first showing a young, well-
conditioned mechanic, sitting in his small, com-
fortably furnished room surrounded by his wife
and three or four children; then followed in order
how, in consequence of a constantly increasing
habit of intemperance, they sink gradually down in
the scale of life, until they go entirely to ruin; his

---

* "The Bottle" was published in 1847.

THE WEDDING DAY. BY GEORGE CRUIKSHANK.

FROM THE "INGOLDSBY LEGENDS."

By permission of Messrs. Macmillan & Co.

sons to penal servitude, and his daughter to degradation, while both his wife and himself die in the
greatest misery and want.

When on the eve of publication, Cruikshank
obtained permission to submit the etchings to
Dr. Blomfield, the then Bishop of London. The

D

Bishop took great interest in looking at the
pictures, and asked many questions as the series
was turned over, expressing his great admiration
in the warmest terms. Then turning and looking
Cruikshank full in the face, he said :

"And am I right in coming to the conclusion,
Mr. Cruikshank, that you are a staunch total
abstainer?"

Cruikshank, in relating this incident to us, said
he never in all his life felt himself in such an
awkward position, for he was obliged to confess
that he did indulge in a little alcohol—occasionally
—and that in great moderation.

"You astonish me, Mr. Cruikshank!—you very
greatly astonish me!" said the Bishop. "For how
a man who is able to depict so forcibly all the
misery, the horrors and degradation arising from
the indulgence in strong drink as you have done,
and himself indulge, even in a moderate degree,
is a mystery which I cannot understand."

"On my way home," continued Cruikshank, "I
felt so inexpressibly ashamed of myself, and how
true the Bishop's remarks were, that I resolved
at once to begin the change which I had long
contemplated, and I subsequently succeeded in
bringing about the desired effect.

"It so happened that a few days after my
interview with the Bishop, I received an invitation
to dine with a gentleman who was famous in
Society for the *recherché* character of his frequent
dinner parties, where the wines were of the
choicest brands and most tempting quality, and

everything was served in the most dainty and perfect fashion.

"Now is the time, I said to myself, to prove my strength of purpose. I was successful in resisting all temptation, and left the house after spending a delightful evening without having tasted a single drop of any other liquid than water.

"The next morning when I went into my study," continued Cruikshank, "I patted my head and said, 'George, old boy, you have done well! You have succeeded, George. You have gained a gigantic triumph, and now you must go on, unflinchingly, and conquer!'—and I did. From that day no alcohol of any description ever crossed my lips, and never shall! NEVER! I'd rather die first!" —here the gallant old fellow posed himself in a dramatic attitude, and throwing out his left arm, and striking his right hand sharply upon his breast, cried in his ringing voice, "FIRE!"

During the latter half of his active life he gave much of his time to the cause of temperance, and no doubt his influence had very great effect. At one of his lectures on the subject at Exeter Hall he held up a brand new "pot" hat of shiniest kind and said, "Ladies and gentlemen, this hat as you see it represents George Cruikshank, the temperance advocate, as he now is." Then throwing the hat to the ground, the brim being undermost, he jumped on the crown, crushing it flat, then holding it up to the audience, shouted, "And this represents George Cruikshank, the drunkard, as he was!"

The old man stuck to his resolution for the remainder of his life, and even on his death-bed, when his medical attendant, the late Sir W. B. Richardson, himself a staunch total abstainer, prescribed that small quantities of brandy should be taken—of course medicinally—he persistently refused to drink it, and so died at an advanced age, firm in the determination which he had formed many years before that not a drop of alcohol of any description should ever pass his lips again.

The first drawings by F. R. Pickersgill that came into our hands to engrave were for " Poems and Pictures," an early "fine art " book, published by J. Burns, of Orchard Street, which contained designs by many of the leading artists of the time, including several by W. Dice, R.A., Cope, R.A., Creswick, R.A., and others. Our connection with Pickersgill—one of the kindest and best of men—soon ripened into a close friendship, and it was to him that we gave the first commission at our own cost for a set of drawings to illustrate " The Life of Christ," desiring to follow the example of Rethel's " Dance of Death," which had just been published in Germany at a very small price.

Our first Part contained six large pictures, printed with a flat tint, the price being one shilling. The second Part, " The Miracles of our Lord," contained the same number of pictures, and at the same price. Our attempt to produce high class art at what was then thought to be a nominal price was not responded to. Other interests were too strong for us ; and although we tried the aid of some first-

THE ADORATION OF THE MAGI. BY F. R. PICKERSGILL, R.A.

REDUCED COPY FROM ONE OF HIS PICTURES FOR "THE LIFE OF CHRIST."

Published for the Brothers Dalziel by Messrs. Chapman & Hall.

class publishers the scheme would not take. We
well remember calling on a well-known publisher of
Scripture work, who, admitting the excellence as
well as the cheapness of the publication, summed
up his refusal to purchase copies with the remark,
" I really cannot afford to set your cask of wine
alongside my barrel of beer."

Pickersgill made drawings for many of the fine
art books produced under our care. He also made
a series of large drawings on the subject of " The
Lord's Prayer," the text of which was paraphrased
in verse by Dean Alford; the book being published
by Messrs. Longman & Co. He also contributed
many beautiful drawings for our Bible Series.

A friend of Pickersgill, the Rev. T. J. Judkin,
an eloquent preacher and clever amateur artist, and
a pupil of Constable's, produced a Volume of Poems
to which many of his artist friends contributed drawings, amongst whom were F. R. Pickersgill, R.A.,
W. Mulready, R.A., Clarkson Stanfield, R.A., E. M.
Ward, R.A., and W. E. Frost, R.A., all of which
we engraved for him.

F. R. Pickersgill, R.A., J. C. Hook, R.A., and
W. E. Frost, R.A., formed a trio in their student
days, working much together, and all illustrating the
same subjects — chiefly passages from Spencer's
" Fairy Queen," and Italian or Venetian History,
basing their style very much upon the Early Italian
School. Later in life a closer tie existed between
two of these artists, Pickersgill marrying Hook's
eldest sister.

Pickersgill told us a somewhat comical experience

Hook had with the Council of "The Art Union of London," who were then procuring a set of drawings on wood by various artists. One subject having been entrusted to Hook, he sent his drawing in, and was asked to call at a stated time, which he did. He saw at once there was something wrong, as

FAIRY DANCE. BY W. E. FROST, R.A.

FROM A BOOK OF POEMS BY THE REV. T. J. JUDKIN.

the gentlemen sat looking at each other. At last one mustered courage to speak, saying :

"We like your drawing very much, Mr. Hook, but—er—doesn't it want colour?—er—where—er—where is your bit of black?"

"I don't want a bit of black," said Hook.

"Oh, but we must have a bit of black. There's Mr. B——, now, he always gives a bit of black."

Hook, feeling fearfully annoyed, took up the drawing, and dipping his finger in a glass of water, smeared it over, saying :

"There, gentlemen, there is your 'bit of black,'" and throwing down the drawing, left the room.

The following short letter from Mr. Hook, which bears upon this subject, will be of interest :

> "TOR VILLA, KENSINGTON,
> "*8th April.*
>
> "DEAR SIRS,—I do not manage wood-drawing well at all—not well enough even to do *me* credit, or I would have done you a drawing with pleasure. I failed some time back in doing one for the Art Union, and recollecting that the blocks they sent me had your name on them, I return them also.
>
> "Believe me, dear Sirs,
> "Yours truly,
> "J. C. HOOK.
>
> "MESSRS. DALZIEL."

In a conversation with Richard Doyle he told us that his father (who was the celebrated "H.B.," a political caricaturist during the thirties and forties) always urged his sons to practise drawing from memory, taking all sorts of subjects; that in their walks they should always try to remember one or more figures they had seen, and immediately on their return home, make the best drawing they could in pen and ink; also to frequent the National Gallery or other important picture exhibitions, remaining in front of any one picture that might attract their attention until they had fairly mastered the subject, and then to make the best recollection of it in pencil or colour as they felt inclined. He highly approved

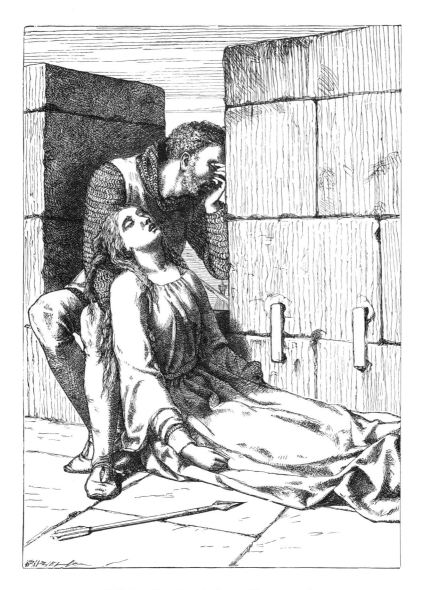

"O breaking heart that will not break,
         Oriana!
O pale, pale face so sweet and meek,
         Oriana!
Thou smilest but thou dost not speak,
And then the tears run down my cheek,
         Oriana!"

—TENNYSON.

BY F. R. PICKERSGILL, R.A.

of this method, and felt he had derived great benefit from the process himself.

Doyle had a facile pencil when once fairly at work, but he was singularly deficient as to the value of time, which appears strange in one who produced so many elaborate drawings; but little reliance could be placed upon him even when working for periodical publications. On one occasion when illustrating a story by Thackeray, the number had to be issued short of certain pictures that had been arranged for. Thackeray was a good deal annoyed and asked Doyle if he could give any reason why he had not done the drawings. He replied in his cool, deliberate manner: "Eh—er—the fact is, I had not got any pencils."

The matter of pencils was always one of some trouble and difficulty with Doyle. The following letter is a fair example of what was a not infrequent occurrence :

"17 CAMBRIDGE TERRACE, HYDE PARK.

"MY DEAR SIRS,—For the reason that *if* I see my way in anything about the realities of the Exhibition, I feel bound to do it for you and Chapman, I must decline Mr. Bogue's proposal.

"I intended to have spoken to you the first time I saw you about pencils for drawing upon wood; do you know a good maker? It is impossible to get anything of the kind at this end of town. If it would not be troubling you too much I would be very much obliged to your getting me half a dozen of the *hardest*, and sending them the next time your messenger comes to me?

"You probably know the best makers, which I do not, having always got my pencils through the *Punch* engravers.

"Yours very truly,

"RICHARD DOYLE."

My dear Sir

I send two large drawings for Jack: and on Tuesday I expect two more. Which will make seven.

On Thursday I leave town for 12 or 14 days, and when I return I hope it will not be too late to send the remainder

Ten, I think was the original number of large drawings we decided upon, but you said you would rather have less of them and more small ones, and consequently I determined on having eight large and twenty or thirty small. I shall not however, be strict as to number, but will do as many as you can give me time to do,

As I may safely say that more than half are now done it would be agreable to me if you will let me have half of the £ S. D. at your earliest convenience.

I remain
very truly yours
Richard Doyle

As I have worked two of the blocks, I have got into a mess with rubbing out I shall be glad if you will send one one or two more.

We gave Doyle a commission to do a Panorama of an Overland Journey to the Great Exhibition of 1851, which it was intended should be published before, or immediately after, the opening day. We need hardly say the drawings were not done to

"Scotland."

FROM "AN OVERLAND JOURNEY TO THE GREAT EXHIBITION OF 1851."

By Richard Doyle.

Published for the Brothers Dalziel by Messrs. Chapman & Hall.

time ; in fact, the last of them was not finished until just on the closing of the Exhibition, consequently the publication was a dead failure.

It is greatly to be regretted that Doyle did not see his way to complete this work at the date agreed upon, and while the great excitement about the Exhibition was at fever heat, for the characteristic humour which is so peculiarly his own, and so cleverly depicted in the various Nationalities forming the Panorama, must have secured for the work a very extensive circulation, and thereby have added greatly to his reputation.

"DEAR SIR,—With regard to the Exhibition procession, I would like to have your opinion as to whether, now the 'Glass House' being open and the public so much seriously occupied with the Exhibition, my drawings will be relished. I don't express any decided opinion now myself, but I put it to you and would like you to ask Mr. Chapman his opinion. I saw the 'procession' that came out a long time ago for the first time the other day to look over, and I really did not know before that the idea was so much the same as mine, and I greatly fear that mine will be thought stale, however original I can make it. It is, in fact, next to impossible to represent any of the countries by other types than those already done in publications already out.

"As far as I myself am concerned—much time as I have lost over this, to me, unfortunate subject—I would rather sacrifice it as lost time than bring out a failure. I cannot expect you, who have also spent some time upon the work, to feel the same.

"What occurred to me, however, was that perhaps the drawings of the 'procession' might be engrafted upon something else, of which it might form a part. I don't see my way, but I throw it out, and would like to have your notion on the subject.

"Very truly yours,

"RICHARD DOYLE."

When Doyle retired from contributing to *Punch*, we gave him a commission to illustrate all the popular Children's Nursery Tales. He expressed himself delighted to undertake the work, and "Jack the Giant Killer" was to be the first. This was done, and published by Cundall and Addy of Bond Street. "The Sleeping Beauty" was the second, but the drawings for this book came so lingeringly to hand that the idea of a series was abandoned, and the blocks were put aside for some time. Those we had, however, were considered so beautiful, and so full of quaint fancy that we decided to enlist the co-operation of J. R. Planche to set new words to them, which he did very charmingly, and the book was published for us by Messrs. G. Routledge and Sons, under the title of "An Old Fairy Tale Told Anew." Those two stories were all Doyle ever did for the series; and their production extended over several years instead of a few months, as would have been the case in the hands of a more business-like artist.

"My dear Sirs,—I send the drawing, which has occupied me almost all the week, and you will see that there is plenty of work in it. The subject is taken from these words in Jack's history: 'He delighted in reading stories about wizards, giants and fairies, and listened eagerly when anybody related the brave deeds of the Knights of the Round Table.'

"It is intended to be the first page of the book (not the title page), and type is to go into the space left in the centre.

"I feel a little anxious about the engraving of the upper half of this drawing, which represents the legend told by the old woman, as I have never yet had that etching style of drawing engraved perfectly to my satisfaction; perhaps that is impossible, but, at all events, as there is plenty of time I shall expect this to be a *chef d'ouvre* of wood engraving, as I certainly look for more than ordinary care in this drawing.

"I have begun another large drawing, which I expect will be ready for you on Monday at six o'clock.

"Very truly yours,

"Richard Doyle."

We cannot help feeling that much excellent work has been lost by Doyle not carrying out this scheme, and fancy what exquisite things he would have made of "Cinderella," "Jack and the Bean Stalk," etc., etc.

FROM "JACK THE GIANT KILLER."

By Richard Doyle.

Published for the Brothers Dalziel by Cundall and Addy.

"17 Cambridge Terrace, Hyde Park.
"*Monday*.

"My dear Sir,—I hear from my brother that you called some days ago wishing to see me. I have settled in town again, after an absence of near three months, and shall be happy to see you at any time. You probably wished to see how the 'Sleeping Beauty' was going on, and I have to relate a misfortune connected therewith; I am sorry to say, several drawings which I had packed in my portmanteau got so rubbed during my journey, that while some were only injured, some were quite spoiled. I have doctored two or three of these, which will be ready for your messenger whenever you will be good enough to send. I shall certainly let you have all the drawings in time to be out for Easter.

"If you could let me have the half of the sum agreed upon for the illustrations, thirty pounds, as early as convenient to you, I should feel much obliged. I think something was said about paying half when half the drawings were done, and therefore I am not strictly entitled to it yet, but forestall the time as it will be a convenience to me to have the money now.

"Yours very truly,

"Richard Doyle."

Notwithstanding his tardiness, so long as Doyle continued to draw upon wood we were in constant communication with him, engraving his productions.

The Arrival at Cologne. "The Passengers Passing their Examination."
From "Brown, Jones and Robinson," by Richard Doyle.

By permission of Messrs. Bradbury & Agnew.

E

Among these may be mentioned many of the illustrations he did for Charles Dickens' Christmas Stories, as well as those he made for Ruskin's charming fairy tale, "The King of the Golden River," Leigh Hunt's "A Jar of Honey from Mount Hylba," and the entire set for "Bird's-Eye Views of Society," published in the *Cornhill Magazine*. We also engraved a large number of his "Brown, Jones and Robinson" pictures. He proposed to us a scheme for doing a companion volume: "Brown, Jones and Robinson in the Highlands of Scotland," but through his dilatory disposition, and the many and varied engagements we had at that time on our hands, the project was not carried out.

Although we had been accustomed for several years, through our connection with Ebenezer Landells and the *Illustrated London News*, to work upon Sir John Gilbert's drawings—perhaps among the very first was a small drawing of "Cupid Delivering a Love Letter," published in an early number of *Punch*—it was not until 1851 that we came into active communication with him. Our first personal interview was to ask him to make two drawings, a title page and frontispiece to "Praise and Principle." He took a small foot rule out of his pocket, measured the size of the two wood blocks, and said, "The price will be thirty-five shillings each, but I could not possibly give them to you to-morrow; but the next morning you may rely on having them." The drawings were duly sent, and with them an account for the

EVENING ON THE LAGO-MAGGIORE.

FROM "BROWN, JONES AND ROBINSON," BY RICHARD DOYLE.

By permission of Messrs. Bradbury & Agnew.

sum named; also a letter to say he had made a mistake in the price, and that all future drawings of the same size and character would be two guineas each. This promptitude, it is worthy of remark, was a striking characteristic of the man, for during the many years that we were in constant intercourse with him, and engraved many hundreds of his drawings, we have no remembrance of him ever being a day behind the time he promised to send in his work.

The drawings for " Praise and Principle " were followed by many sets of illustrations, generally eight in number, for books issued by the Messrs. Routledge.

As an example of his peculiar method of book keeping in those early days the following letter will be interesting:

"VANBURGH PARK,
"BLACKHEATH, *June 2nd.*

"DEAR SIRS,—I am now going out to send the drawings by the Parcels Delivery Company. Will you kindly let me know that you have received them safely?

"My charge for the four is twelve guineas. As I have no account with any one now, and therefore no book wherein to enter such a transaction, only a pencil mem. stuck into a frame on the wall, I will ask you at your convenience to let me have a cheque for the amount.

"Very truly yours,
"JOHN GILBERT.

"MESSRS. DALZIEL."

Early in 1852 we were commissioned by Messrs. Ingram and Cook, who had then added a book publishing business to their other operations, to engrave the pictures for an édition de luxe of

"His mother she prepared a feast—
Great stores of venison and wine."

"The Salamandrine."—Dr. Charles Mackay.

By Sir John Gilbert, R.A., P.R.W.S.

By permission of Messrs. George Routledge & Sons.

Dr. Charles Mackay's beautiful and fantastical poem "The Salamandrine," which Sir John Gilbert had undertaken to illustrate; and it may be confidently said that of the thousands of drawings which he afterwards made he never surpassed the charm and grace of his manipulative skill as shown in this exquisitely decorated volume. The book was very beautifully got up and most perfectly printed. Of our labour and part in the production, perhaps it may be sufficient to quote a short note Dr. Mackay wrote to us on the subject:

"*December 27th, 1852.*

"MY DEAR SIR,—I cannot but express to you and your brother how gratified and obliged I feel for the care you have bestowed upon the illustrations for 'The Salamandrine.' I think they are triumphs of the art of wood engraving, and I sincerely hope that your efforts will be amply rewarded not only in present and future reputation but in pecuniary advantages.

"The *Morning Chronicle* of Saturday contains a fitting tribute to your exertions, and it is likely, I think, that other papers will follow in the same strain.

"Believe me,
"Ever yours truly,
"CHARLES MACKAY.

"E. DALZIEL, ESQ."

Following "The Salamandrine," began the most important works of our lives, and it was through the enterprise of Messrs. Routledge and Warne that we were enabled to produce so long a list of "Fine Art Books," some of them on commission, and many others entirely on our own responsibility. These also brought us many important commissions from such houses as Messrs. Longman & Co., W. Blackwood & Son, Smith, Elder & Co., J. Nisbet & Co., Appleton & Co., New York, Roberts Brothers, Boston, and several other publishers of high standing both in England and America.

LUCY GRAY, OR SOLITUDE.

" To-night will be a stormy night,
You to the town must go,
And take the lantern, child, to light
Your mother through the snow."
—WILLIAM WORDSWORTH.

BY SIR JOHN GILBERT, R.A., P.R.W.S.

An important feature in Sir John Gilbert's practice in this branch of his art was his marvellous power of design, and wonderful dexterity in execution. On one occasion during the progress of his work he spoke of a drawing that had given him some trouble. He said, " Would you believe it, sir, I was so dissatisfied with it that I absolutely rubbed it out." He was asked one day whether he ever made an alteration on any other drawing for " The Salamandrine." He replied, " Was there ever any evidence of such a thing?"

But the greatest work of his that passed through our hands was Staunton's " Shakespeare," also published by Messrs. Routledge, the publication extending over four years. Vast as it was, he never disappointed us as to time, and when we take into consideration the number and elaborate character of the drawings, his regularity in sending them in was really surprising. The system adopted was to leave the tailpieces at the end of each Act to be drawn according to the size of the spaces left on the pages, and it was our custom to send a set of sheets of a Play down to him by special messenger with the understanding that he was to bring the drawings, four or five, as the case might be, back with him the same evening, which he always did : many of them being so elaborately and so carefully finished as to prove that Gilbert literally had the subjects at " his fingers' ends."

The following letters are of interest as expressing Gilbert's opinion and impression on seeing the first number of this important work :

KING LEAR.

ONE OF SIR JOHN GILBERT'S EIGHT HUNDRED AND
THIRTY-TWO ILLUSTRATIONS TO THE
WORKS OF SHAKESPEARE.

"BLACKHEATH,
                "*Wednesday Evening.*

"DEAR SIRS,—I have looked at, examined, and criticised the first number of 'Shakespeare' to that extent that positively I hardly know what opinion to express of the first fruits of our labours.

"The Frontispieces will be an immense addition; without them it seems that there are not enough pictures for the money—and yet, eighteen cuts such as these are is surely a good shilling's worth. It appears to me— *mind*, I don't feel quite convinced of it, for, as I said before, I've so over and over considered it that I get quite confused—that large cuts are wanted, *fewer* and *larger*. What do you think of two cuts to each act, and those, ten in all, larger, keeping the little ones for tailpieces, where necessary to have a tailpiece?

"Turn this over in your mind, and if you think it desirable, consult Messrs. Routledge. I cannot help thinking ten cuts, about two-thirds the size of the space occupied by the type, would have a greater effect, and I should say cost no more than the sum laid down.

          *   *   *   *   *   *   *   *

"You desired to have my opinion of the number, but I fear you will say, 'Here is no opinion at all.'

            "Believe me to be, dear Sirs,
                "Yours truly,
                    "JOHN GILBERT."

On the completion of the first volume, he says:

"Mr. Routledge and Mr. Warne both wrote to me expressing their great satisfaction with the last number, and I suppose it must be considered a good shilling's worth. You know how I appreciate your labours; there are cuts in the last number that cannot be exceeded, and looking at the volume, I think, for general even goodness of style in engraving, it has never been excelled."

That the printing of some of our books was not at all times faultless, the following note from Sir John Gilbert will testify. In acknowledging a volume of India proofs, he says:

KING LEAR AND FOOL IN A STORM.

LEAR. *"Blow, winds, and crack your cheeks! rage! blow!*
You cataracts, and hurricanoes, spout
Till you have drench'd our steeples."
—SHAKESPEARE.

BY SIR JOHN GILBERT, R.A., P.R.W.S.

By permission of Messrs. George Routledge & Sons.

"I write to acknowledge a volume of proofs. Its size and thickness impressed me, and I don't well know how sufficiently to thank you for having had the proofs bound up with such care and taste. I can only say that I thank you very much for it, and that it will be highly valued by me. I had no idea of the magnificent style you had intended to get it up. Comparing these proofs with the impressions in the volume of poems, I am more than ever impressed that the printer has not done his part properly: the difference is immense.

"Believe me, very truly,

"JOHN GILBERT."

About this time W. Harrison Ainsworth was editing "Bentley's Miscellany," and published some of his own works through that journal, Sir John Gilbert making the illustrations to "The Lancaster Witches," which were entrusted to us for engraving and printing. In sending a cheque, Ainsworth wrote :

"I have much pleasure in sending you a cheque in payment of your account for the engraving and printing of the designs, all of which have my entire satisfaction."

Again, in another letter accompanying a set of drawings by Gilbert, illustrating "The Constable of the Tower," he says :

"I have always thought Mr. Gilbert's illustrations to 'Lancaster Witches' as in every way charmingly engraved, and I have no doubt the present cuts will equal them, if not surpass them, in beauty.

"Ever yours truly,

"W. HARRISON AINSWORTH."

While the illustrations to "Shakespeare" were in progress we had two sets of engraver's burnished India proofs taken by skilled hands, under our own special care, before the wood blocks were delivered

Thursday Evening.

My dear Sir,

I have just had a glance over the number of the
Shakspere just issued, and cannot resist writing to
ask me to express the very great gratification
it has given me. You have indeed done your part
of the work nobly; it does you the greatest credit
and confirms me in the belief I always have had
that no one can engrave my drawings like you
can. I have written to thank Routledge & Co for
sending me the [...] — and believe me to be yours

G. Cruikshank

to the printer. One set, we are pleased to say, is now the property of the British Museum, where they will remain in all their original beauty.

Sir John Gilbert died at his house, Vanburgh Park Road, Blackheath, on October 5th, 1897, in his 81st year.

His brother, Mr. Frederick Gilbert, writing on his death, says, "My brother, Sir John, had a long and distressing illness, but we are thankful to think not a very painful one—he died very peacefully."

A friend of Sir John's called upon him a few months before his death and found him hard at work, and making a favourable remark about the picture he was engaged upon, the veteran replied, quite seriously, "Well, yes! I think I'm improving."

"And I am told, Sir John," continued the friend, "that you have never painted from the living model."

Sir John turned his head, with an amused look about the eyes, saying, "Well, to tell you the truth, I cannot remember the time when I did so."

The writer of a highly appreciative article in the *Magazine of Art*, says, "Though Sir John Gilbert painted art in every branch, it is only in one, and that not in the public estimation the one by which he defies the rivalry of all comers, that he showed himself head and shoulders above the draughtsmen of his time. . . . Distinguished as he was as a painter, it is in virtue of his achievements in black and white that he takes his

LEAR FANTASTICALLY DRESSED WITH FLOWERS.

BY SIR JOHN GILBERT, R.A., P.R.W.S.

By permission of Messrs. George Routledge & Sons.

place among the few masters, not of his age and country only, but of all time, who through the medium of the hand and printing press have ranged themselves among the highest. . . . He may be voted old-fashioned for the moment, but real art rises superior to mode or vogue in taste : it has time upon its side.

"Added to innumerable illustrations made for the *London Journal,* it is estimated that Sir John Gilbert made at least 30,000 drawings for the *Illustrated London News.**   He sent 50 pictures to the Royal Academy, 20 to the British Artists, 40 to the Royal Water Colour Society, 40 to the British Institute, and produced about 270 works which have never been exhibited.   Added to this stupendous list of works he contributed 110 drawings to the Illustrated Edition of 'Longfellow's Poems,' 50 to Dr. Charles Mackay's 'Salamandrine,' 832 to Staunton's 'Shakespeare,' several to 'Lays of the Holy Land,' 'The Book of Job,' and 'Wordsworth's Poems,' as well as a liberal contribution to the long series of books known as 'Dalziel's Fine Art Books.'"

In referring to Gilbert's book illustrations a recent writer says, "There is no sign of haste, though many are sketchy ; still, there is nothing which suggests that greater excellence would have attended greater elaboration."

---

* Here we think the writer of the article has over estimated the number, as Sir John had for many years before his death entirely severed his connection with the *Illustrated London News,* as well as all other journalistic work.

CHAPTER III.

Sir J. E. Millais, P.R.A., Holman Hunt, Dante G. Rossetti, Arthur Hughes, Millais' "Parables of Our Lord," Sir J. Noel Paton, P.R.S.A., Sir John Tenniel, Etc.

MUCH has been written about "The Golden Period of Illustration" as it existed in the early Sixties, represented by wood engraving and the admirable drawings done for that process by such artists as Sir John Millais, Fred Walker, A. Boyd Houghton, Dante G. Rossetti, G. J. Pinwell, Sir E. J. Poynter, Lord Leighton, Sir E. Burne-Jones, F. Sandys, and other notable artists.

Our opportunities were favourable. We were equally fortunate in being so intimately connected with men possessing such exceptional talent, and it must ever be a great satisfaction to us that we were in a position to avail ourselves of their brilliant ability.

Our co-operation with Sir John Millais began about midway in the fifties, when, at his request, Moxon, the publisher, brought one of the Tennyson drawings for us to engrave, and continued for many years, during which time a large majority of the drawings he made for wood engraving were entrusted to us. These included his work for the *Cornhill Magazine*, *Good Words*, and the majority of those he did for other serial publications, including the illustrations to Anthony Trollope's "Orley Farm," "The Small House at Allington," and "Framley Parsonage." This artistic association only ceased when he discontinued doing this class of work.

F

During the entire time we gave the most perfect satisfaction to Millais, who frequently expressed himself in the warmest, and to us extremely flattering, terms of appreciation.

We subsequently discovered that it was to Richard Doyle we were indebted for our introduction to Millais, who was then living at Bowerswell, Perth, where Doyle was on a visit, and noticing the delicate character of a drawing he was at work upon said he believed the Dalziels were the only engravers who could do justice to such elaborate manipulation. Upon this Millais requested Moxon to place the drawings in our hands, and so satisfied was he with our first performance, that all the remaining drawings he made for this edition of "Tennyson's Poems" were given to us.

Previous to Mr. Moxon entrusting Millais' drawings to us, he had placed all the subjects with the different artists, but found great difficulty in getting the work from them. He gave us a list of those waited for, and placed the completion of the engravings in our hands, asking us to look up the artists, which brought us in close communication with those engaged upon the work.

He also asked us to superintend the printing of the book, which was being done by Messrs. Bradbury and Evans, who certainly bestowed the greatest care upon its production, but no sheet was sent to Press until we had signed it as "approved." The number printed was 10,000 copies, which were done at the old hand press, for at that time cylinder machine work was not considered good

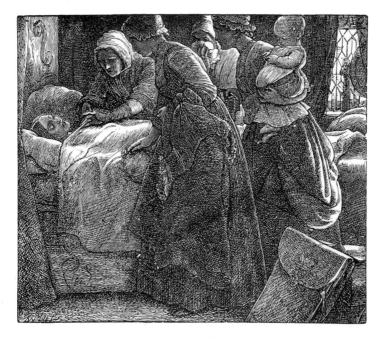

THE LORD OF BURLEIGH.
TENNYSON.

BY SIR J. E. MILLAIS, P.R.A.

By permission of Messrs. Macmillan & Co.

enough : but all that has long been changed—the finest and most elaborate work being now produced in this way.

This edition will always be known as " Moxon's Tennyson," and will stand out as a landmark in the history of book illustration. In the work of the younger men engaged on it, beyond the extreme beauty of their designs, there was an evidence of earnestness to search after truth that went so deep into nature as to give the work a stamp of superiority : and this advance in art—for it was an advance—we endeavoured to follow and to promote to the best of our power.

Locksley Hall proof

The outline of the daughters head
is too thick from this unforgiven
I cannot see the mouth but
will wait for the next, the nostril
is too large , , and the
mothers' face is too full of little
fine lines, take away
the fuzzy lines indicating the
upperlip — Clear the eye
enlarging the upper lid by making
this line of the eye less thick
bad / right
There are some little scratches on
the fingers holding the envelope

which may be taken out,
In this ladies of the daughters
hands on her side, there are
some black veins which may also
be eradicated — There are
other little corrections if you compare
these touched proofs, with others
as the blocks are — I wish now
I am very hard at work painting
but will attend to the Coleridge
& Byron designs at my first
leisure — Hoping to hear from
you soon believe me yours very truly

Dalziel Brothers. John Everett Millais

The volume was published by Mr. Moxon at
£1 11s. 6d., but the public did not respond as had
been expected, consequently a large stock was left
on hand. These were sold to Messrs. Routledge and
Co, and, with the stock, the entire set of the wood
blocks went also. The price of the volume was
reduced to £1 1s., and it sold out immediately.
On this success Messrs. Routledge wished to produce
a new edition, but Tennyson's terms were too high to
leave any margin of profit to the publisher. This
doubtless was the cause of the book being so long
out of print ; but the property having since passed
into the hands of Messrs. Macmillan they have
reproduced this very interesting book.

On November 23rd, 1856, Mr. Holman Hunt, on
receiving the proof of a drawing he had made for
Moxon's edition, writes :

"I find the proof of the last design for 'Oriana' very
satisfactory, giving the character of the drawing with great
truth."

Although we were in communication with Dante
Gabriel Rossetti at an earlier date, when we engraved
a small drawing* which he made in illustration to
a poem, "The Maids of Elfin-Mere," by William
Allingham, published by Bell and Daldy, in a volume

---

* This drawing was a remarkable example of the artist being altogether
unacquainted with the necessary requirements in making a drawing on
wood for the engraver's purposes. In this Rossetti made use of wash,
pencil, coloured chalk, and pen and ink, producing a very nice effect,
but the engraved reproduction of this many tinted drawing, reduced
to the stern realities of black and white by printers' ink, failed to
satisfy him. Indeed, Rossetti appears to have made up his mind that
it would be a failure, for in writing to his friend Allingham, after

FROM "THE TALKING OAK."

TENNYSON.

BY SIR J. E. MILLAIS, P.R.A.

By permission of Messrs. Macmillan & Co.

entitled, "Day and Night Songs"—Rossetti's artist co-workers in this book were J. E. Millais and Arthur Hughes, all the drawings being engraved

---

explaining the difficulty he had experienced in making the drawing, he says: "As to the engraving, I suppose it is hardly possible that I can be satisfied."

It is further interesting to note in Mr. Malcolm Bell's work of "Sir E. Burne-Jones: A Record and Review," that on seeing the engraving, "Elfin-Mere," it revealed to him for the first time the "World of radiant, many-coloured lights; of dim, mysterious shadows, of harmonies of form of line; that far-off World of Art into which he has made his way and brought back visions of delight to show his fellow man."

by ourselves—we did not come in contact with him again until we received the following letter :

"17 ORANGE GROVE, BATH.

"MY DEAR SIRS,—I have just had a note from Mr. Moxon sent to me here, by which I learn that you are cutting a drawing of mine, and that it will soon be finished. Will you kindly send me the proof *here* (to the above address) and I will at once retouch it and send it back to London. I have been lately admiring your work in the 'Poets of the 19th Century,' and can only hope for a rendering equal to what Millais has there had at your hands.

"Yours very truly,

"D. G. ROSSETTI."

The Millais drawings here alluded to are those made to illustrate passages from Byron and Coleridge, mentioned later on. His own was the St. Cecillia which Rossetti did for the "Illustrated Tennyson." *

It would be obviously out of place for us to comment upon the difference in treatment which we gave, and that of other engravers who were entrusted to operate upon some of the drawings he made for this book, or to remark upon the comparisons of certain critics writing upon the subject ; we can only affirm that Mr. Rossetti expressed himself both verbally and by letter as being well pleased with our work. Writing on the receipt of two finished proofs, he says :

* Of this drawing, the St. Cecillia, his brother, Mr. W. M. Rossetti, writes : "It must be said that himself only and not Tennyson was his guide. He drew just what he chose, taking from the author's text nothing more than a hint and an opportunity. The illustration to St. Cecillia puzzled Tennyson not a little, and he had to give up the problem of what it had to do with his verses"

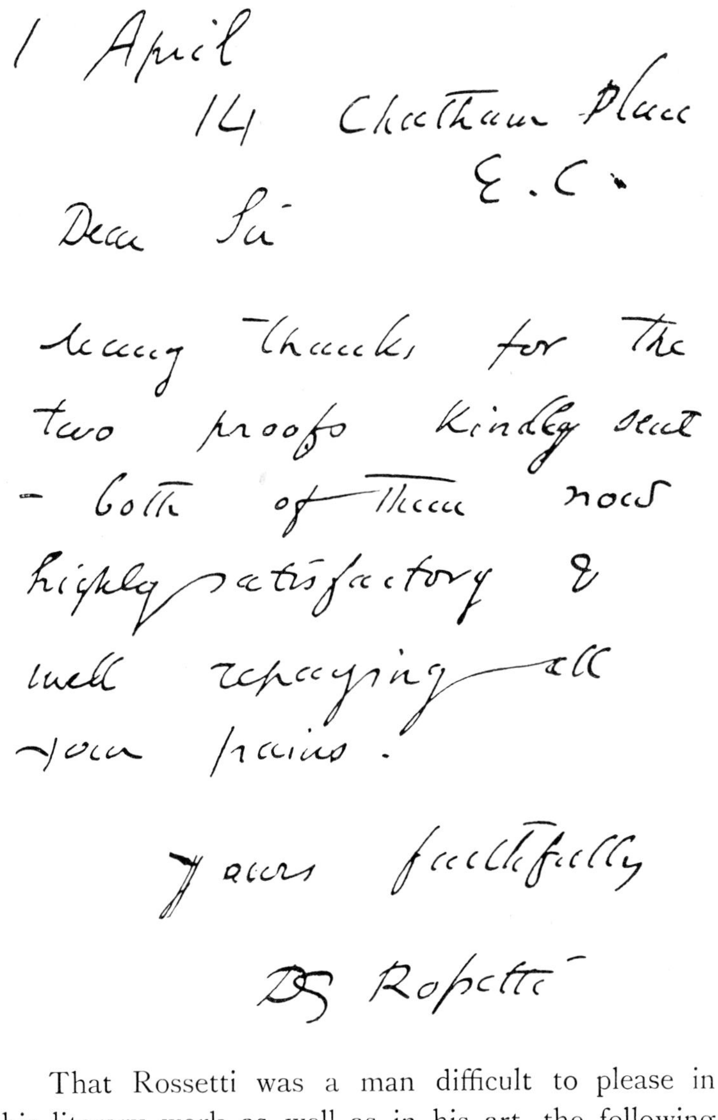

1 April
14 Chatham Place
E.C.

Dear Sir

Many thanks for the two proofs kindly sent — both of them now highly satisfactory & well repaying all your pains.

Yours faithfully

DG Rossetti

That Rossetti was a man difficult to please in his literary work as well as in his art, the following is an apt illustration :

In one of the " Allingham letters," he says :

" I lately heard from Aubrey de Vere with a request to my sister and self to contribute something to a verse collection.

THE BALLAD OF ORIANA.

TENNYSON.

BY HOLMAN HUNT.

By permission of Messrs. Macmillan & Co.

We looked up scraps and expected proofs, but these come not, and I imagine that the result, when in type, will be the usual incentive to Blasphemy."

Mr. W. M. Rossetti, writing of his brother's social peculiarities, says:

"He assumed the easy attitude of one born to dominate —to know his own place and to set others in theirs. He was a genial despot, good natured, hearty and unassuming in manner, and only tenacious upon the question at issue."

Though we never had any personal interview with Rossetti's sister, Miss Christina Rossetti, we had considerable correspondence with this gifted

ST. CECILLIA.

THE "PALACE OF ART."

TENNYSON.

BY DANTE G. ROSSETTI.

lady, extending over several years, she having written
some short poems which helped to adorn the pages
of one or more of our Fine Art Books. We
also published her charming little Nursery Rhyme
Book, "Sing Song," which was very tastefully illustrated by Arthur Hughes. The manuscript of this
book was somewhat of a curiosity in its way. On
each page, above the verse, was a slight pen sketch,
drawn by Miss Rossetti, suggesting the subject to
illustrate, but of these Mr. Hughes made very little
use, and only in two instances actually followed the

sketch. The book was published on our behalf by Messrs. George Routledge & Co.

On one occasion when Mr. Arthur Hughes sent in some of the drawings which he had made, one of the pages of manuscript was missing, and on this being pointed out to him he sent the following note :

"July 31, '71.

"Dear Messrs. Dalziel,—I am sure that I put in the rhyme of 'Dancing on the hill tops.' I am very careful with them—going two or three times through them before packing up. I don't remember which was 45, but the four figures representing the Seasons is to the poem of the Months, beginning 'January, cold, desolate'; and as well as I can remember the poem for the drawing of a man with fagot and basket meeting his child— it goes thus :

> ' Dancing on the hill tops,
>   Singing in the valleys,
>   Laughing with the echoes,
>   Merry little Alice.
>   If her father's cottage
>   Turned into a palace,
>   And he owned the hill tops
>   And the flowering valleys,
>   She'd be none the happier—
>   Happy little Alice.'

—and had a pencil sketch at top of a child on a pointed hill.

"I am just about finishing a batch of these—belonging to last week, alas !—but I am also finishing the frontispiece of the Carols. These shall come very soon.

> "Believe me,
>   "Faithfully yours,
>   "Arthur Hughes."

We had for a long time cherished the idea of doing an important series of illustrations to "The Parables of Our Lord." This occupied much

HALLELUJAH

THE "SUNDAY MAGAZINE."

BY ARTHUR HUGHES.

Published by Mr. Alexander Strahan.

anxious thought and careful consideration, for we felt it would be useless attempting the subject unless the drawings were made by an artist of acknowledged high-class ability. We found our chief difficulty in fixing upon one capable of treating the subject with sufficient dignity, and at the same time likely to avoid the old conventional style in which at that time Biblical art was treated. As many of Sir John Millais' charming drawings had been passing through our hands—among others we would mention some exceptionally beautiful work illustrating selected passages from poems by Byron and Coleridge, as well as his exquisite drawing of "The Finding of Moses"—it seemed to us that he would be a safe man to consult on the subject, and likely to give us something more original in treatment than any other artist who was doing this class of work.

Millais entered warmly into the subject and very readily undertook the commission, as the accompanying letter will show :

"BOWERSWELL, PERTH,

"*13 August, '57.*

"DEAR SIRS,—I shall be very glad to accept your offer, but you must give me time. One great inducement for me to undertake these illustrations is the fact that the book will be entirely illustrated by me alone. The subject is quite to my liking ; you could not have chosen anything more congenial to my desire. I would set about them immediately if you will send me some blocks. Will you send me a list of the Parables, or leave it to me? I would prefer the former. There is so much labour in these drawings that I trust you will give me my own time, otherwise I could not undertake the commission. I should make it a labour of love like yourselves.

"Yours very truly,

"JOHN EVERETT MILLAIS."

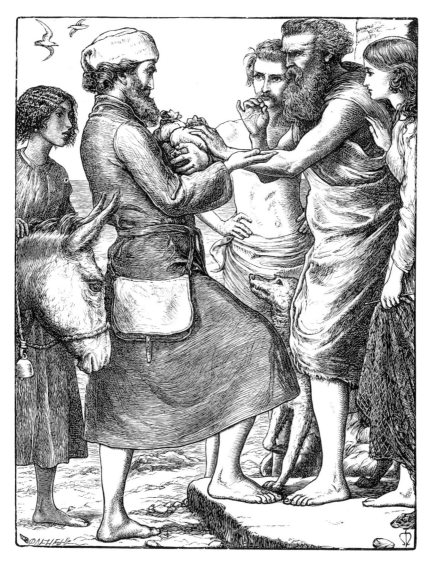

THE PEARL OF GREAT PRICE.

FROM "THE PARABLES OF OUR LORD."

BY SIR J. E. MILLAIS, P.R.A.

Monday   Bowerswell
                  Perth

Dear Dalziel,

At last I have
finished "The Pearl of great
price — you will at once see there
is a tremendous lot of work in
it — & I have put a little
more white in parts than
perhaps is good — but I could
not help it — as I require to
alter a good deal —
I know very well you will give it
all your attention & after that
that you have done I feel
sure it will be rendered a

facsimile = The head of Lucy Robarts is just that I wanted which is very fortunate as I could not suggest alterations —

Yours sincerely
John E. Millais

Messrs Dalziel Brothers

Millais produced several of the drawings very promptly, but, as time went on and he became more popular—the demand for his pictures daily increasing—longer intervals gradually took place between the delivery of the drawings, and it was not until the end of 1864 that the last was sent in. Even then he had only made twenty drawings out of thirty, which he at first undertook to do. At the same time he requested us to release him from the remainder of the agreement, and to this we had no choice but to comply, though we did so very reluctantly, feeling that the world of art would be so much the poorer.

In 1862 we accepted an offer from Mr. Alexander Strahan, and twelve of these pictures were published in *Good Words Magazine.* Later, in 1864, the entire series was published for us in book form by George Routledge & Sons. But we are sorry to say they did not receive that liberal recognition from either the public or the critics which their undoubted excellence ought to have commanded.

When we conceived the idea of doing an Illustrated Bible, of which we will have much to say further on, Millais was one of the first artists we consulted on the subject. He warmly approved of the project, and promised his most hearty and liberal co-operation ; but like many other equally hearty promises from artists of note, they were never fulfilled, not, we are sure, from any want of sympathy with the subject, but owing entirely to the pressure of other engagements. At last his undertaking on this work simmered down to a positive promise of one drawing, and that to be "Adam and Eve in the Garden of Eden," but though he was often solicited, and always promised to set about it immediately, he never made the drawing, nor do we know that he went so far as to make even the slightest rough sketch of a design for it. To us this was an inexpressible disappointment, as without that picture it was obviously impossible to commence the publication.

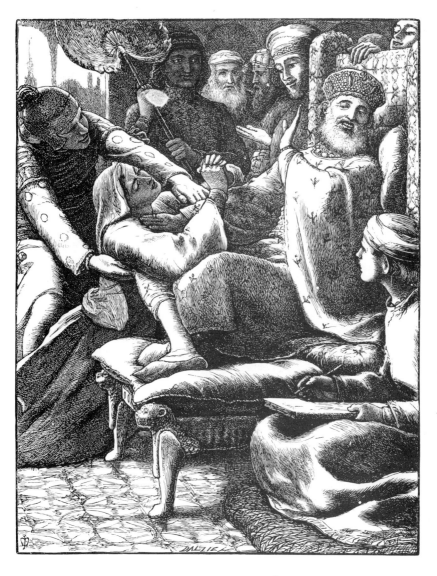

THE UNJUST JUDGE.*

FROM "THE PARABLES OF OUR LORD."

BY SIR J. E. MILLAIS, P.R.A.

By permission of Messrs. Herbert Virtue & Co., Ltd.

* Sir John Millais, in his letter on page 100, calls this the "Importunate Widow."

Borrowash Gutta.
                    14 Jany. 59.
Dear Sir.

            Nothing can be more

exquisitely rendered than the

"Importunate Widow". There are

two or three little trifles wh. I

will talk you when I come up.

It appears to me even better cuts

than any other I have worsten

you have only to show it to any

artist, & he will at once see

how it is executed — The two

I am about are the Ten

Virgins". I will try & send

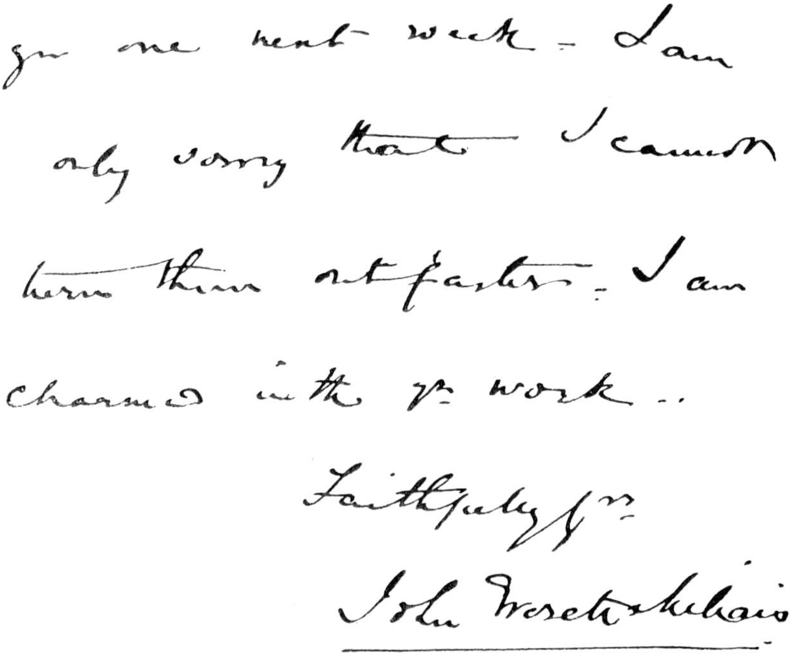

[handwritten letter facsimile]

you one next week — I am

only sorry that I cannot

turn them out faster — I am

charmed with your work ..

Faithfully yr

John Everett Millais

This, with many other similar disappointments of help which we had confidently relied upon, caused the project to hang fire, until at last, in 1880, we resolved to abandon the idea of an Illustrated Bible, and publish some of the engravings we had made in a folio under the title of " Dalziel's Bible Gallery."

That our difficulties in carrying out the elaborate project we had formed began at an early date, the following extract from a letter by Sir John Millais, dated February 8th, 1863, will show :

"There is a decided move in the matter of 'The Bible.' Hunt, Watts, and Leighton will not, I expect, work for you, as they say they are, with me, in honour bound to work for the publisher who first made the proposal.   There can be no doubt but that we should, in such a case, work together.

"Yours very faithfully,

"JOHN EVERETT MILLAIS."

The "publisher who first made the proposal" here referred to was Mr. Joseph Cundall, who was not at that time in business as a publisher, but had formed a project of publishing an "Illustrated Bible." His progress in the matter merely consisted in his having commissioned the several artists named by Millais, with two or three others, while his actual purchase was three small drawings of minor importance. These, with his "priority of claim," we subsequently purchased from him. We never used the drawings, however, not considering them favourable specimens.

In a letter, which is without date, showing how earnestly Millais laboured and how anxious he was to give his most perfect work in producing the charming series of illustrations to "The Parables of Our Lord," he says:

"I send off by post the Parable of 'The Leaven which the woman hid in the three measures of meal'; she is mixing the leaven in the last of the three.   The girl at the back I have made near the oven with one of the loaves, and the other rests against the wall of the window."

Further on in the same letter he writes:

"It is almost unnecessary for me to say that I cannot produce these quickly even if supposing I give *all my* time to them.   They are separate pictures, and so I exert myself to the utmost to make them as complete as possible.   I can do ordinary illustrations as quickly as most men, but these designs can scarcely be regarded

THE LEAVEN.

FROM "THE PARABLES OF OUR LORD."

BY SIR J. E. MILLAIS, P.R.A.

By permission of Messrs. Herbert Virtue & Co., Ltd.

in the same light—each Parable I illustrate perhaps a dozen times before I fix, and the 'Hidden Treasures' I have altered on the wood at least six times. The manipulation of the drawings takes much less time than the arrangement, although you cannot but see how carefully they are executed. Believe me, I will not again halt in the work, but will supply you regularly, although I may occasionally delay in the production. I know you will take every care in the cutting, so I will not say anything about that. I enclose with the block a few remarks.

"Ever yours truly,

"John Everett Millais.

"I suppose you have nearly completed the 'Five Foolish Virgins.' I am always anxious to get the proofs."

Sir John was at all times ready to help a brother or sister artist, and avoid as far as possible running in competition, as the following few lines will show.

In a letter dated February 8th, 1863, he writes:

"I forgot to ask you not to publish the 'Lost Sheep' amongst the Parables in *Good Words*, as I have had a letter from Mrs. Blackburn stating that she had a drawing for the paper of the same subject, and wishing me to keep back that illustration if it did not interfere with the arrangement. I suppose it will make no difference to you, so please withhold it from the set devoted to *Good Words*."

In reference to the engraving of " The Lord of Burleigh" he says :

"Perth,

"*December 10, '56.*

"My dear Sirs,—I received the proofs this afternoon and am quite satisfied with the cutting, which is perfect. I mention a few corrections, or rather additions, which I think will improve them. As I have omitted to add my monogram to the other drawings I should like it cut out of the snow in the illustration to the 'Old Year.' The only improvement I see is a want of softness in some of the outlines, which may be reduced or made to look more tender. I have written in pencil such faults as strike me may be easily remedied.

"The more I have looked into the cutting of both these (but especially the 'Burleigh') the more delighted I am with the rendering. I wish you would send me a good proof of each of them, as I have all the others.

"Again thanking you for the evident care you have taken in rendering my drawings,

"Believe me,

"Ever yours truly,

"JOHN EVERETT MILLAIS."

Millais, on returning proofs which we had submitted for his touching or approval, invariably made such favourable remarks on our portion of the work as the following :

"*November 6, '63.*

"The proofs you sent me are perfectly satisfactory. 'The Good Shepherd' doesn't require anything, and the other only wants a touch on the face. Next to the King is a little coarse in the shadow : make it a little less scratchy."

In reply to a letter of ours asking for a further supply of "Parable" drawings, Mrs. Millais writes :

"BOWERSWELL,

"*August 9th.*

"DEAR SIR,—I am very sorry to write to you instead of packing up for you some wood drawings. Mr. Millais has begged me to write to you, as he says he is ashamed of himself, but he has felt such a disinclination to turn to that kind of drawing at present, when he is painting out of doors, that he must beg you to have patience with him. Several times as he has got designs and drawings ready, I have got him to sit down to them, but he rose up disgusted and feeling incapable. He goes to London next week but returns in a few days. He declares he will then set to work, so we must hope the fit will have come on for work of the kind in which you are interested. In the meantime he has nothing nearly ready, if he would only begin again, but he is at work all day, and in the evening too tired. Next week the young ladies he is painting from leave, and he will be free to turn to something else.

"With best regards,

"Believe me, yours truly,

"EFFIE MILLAIS."

Mrs. Millais, writing on another occasion to account for the non-delivery of drawings, says:

"BOWERSWELL, PERTH,

"*November 26th.*

"He is very sorry not to answer your letter about the Parables. He says, at this season, that he is always occupied on his pictures, and that although he can occasionally do drawings on the wood at odd times, that he cannot attempt to do the Parables, which are, as you know, much finer work. He is anxious to make that work as perfect as possible, and when he does one or more he puts his painting aside for the time. He cannot do that during the winter and spring, and therefore begs you to have patience with him, as he will work at them whenever he has sufficient leisure. He is well aware how anxious you are to have the work finished. I am sure he is also. But he often makes designs, and continues to improve them until he is quite satisfied that it is as good as he can make it, and this takes a long time.

"Very truly yours,

"EFFIE MILLAIS."

On our sending Millais complete copies of "The Parables" he wrote the following letter:

"7 CROMWELL PLACE,

"SOUTH KENSINGTON,

"*5th Dec., 1863.*

"DEAR DALZIEL,—I am quite *delighted* with the Book, and I think you will find the public will slowly and surely appreciate it. Six copies will not quite do for the friends I have promised it to, but will be enough for the present. I desired to send copies

"*Now, Randolph, tell thy tidings,*
However sharp they be."

"Edinburgh, after Flodden."—Aytoun.

FROM "LAYS OF THE SCOTTISH CAVALIERS."

By Sir J. Noel Paton, P.R.S.A.

By permission of Messrs. William Blackwood & Sons.

to men who will very much forward the sale—such as Tennyson, Layard, Thackeray, Leech, etc. If you could send me another six I think that would do amply. I will not forget 'The Arabian Nights.' The only fault, I think, in the Book is that in the middle there are too many blank pages, but I suppose that could not be helped.

"Sincerely yours,

"John Everett Millais."

The following is an extract from the Preface to the first edition of the book :

"Mr. Millais made his first drawing to illustrate the Parables in August, 1857, and the last in October, 1863. Thus he has been able to give that care and consideration to his subjects which the beauty as well as the importance of 'The Parables' demanded, for the work has extended over a period of six years."

During the years from 1858 to 1863 we engraved several grand drawings by Sir J. Noel Paton in illustration to a fine art edition of Professor Aytoun's " Lays of the Scottish Cavaliers," published by Messrs. Blackwood of Edinburgh. In a letter, dated October 8th, 1858, he says :

"33 George Street, Edinburgh.

"Dear Sirs,—Judging from your work in the 'Tennyson,' and from proofs now before me, I can with perfect security and confidence recommend the Messrs. Blackwood to entrust you with as many of my drawings as you care to undertake. Indeed I did so in those very words when, a few months ago, we were discussing this question of engraving, and I am quite ready to repeat my recommendation, though having, by my own desire, left the choice of engravers entirely in the hands of Messrs. Blackwood.

"I remain, Gentlemen,

"Yours very truly,

"J. Noel Paton."

"Yet a black and murky battlement
Lay resting on the hill."

"The Execution of Montrose."—AYTOUN.

FROM "LAYS OF THE SCOTTISH CAVALIERS."

BY SIR J. NOEL PATON, P.R.S.A.

By permission of Messrs. William Blackwood & Sons.

On returning parcels of touched proofs, he wrote the following letters :

"33 George Street, Edinburgh,
August 22, 1862.

"Gentlemen,—I herewith return the three printed proofs touched upon, and by that you will kindly do your best to carry out the alterations indicated.

"The last proofs sent (eight in number) will be forwarded to Mr. Simpson to-day. They are, upon the whole, very satisfactory, though all, more or less, requiring *careful overhauling*, though through no shortcoming of yours, as the drawings have been wonderfully rendered. I would more especially mention as worthy of all praise, as specimens of engraving, 'The Melrose,' and the interior with figures, and the suit of armour. The latter is certainly very perfect.

"Your kind offer of a proof of Mr. Houghton's beautiful design, and your beautiful Engraving of the long-haired Lady with Children, I cannot refuse ; though in what I said in my last, I merely meant to indicate the desire, which so many must feel, that high class things of that sort could be got by *themselves* and printed in a manner worthy of their excellence—they are generally so indifferently printed in the Periodicals in which they appear and *dis*-appear.

"In haste.

"Very faithfully yours,

"J. Noel Paton.

"Messrs. Dalziel.'

"Absence from Town, and other causes, has prevented me from acknowledging more promptly 15 proofs of your engravings for the 'Lays of the Scottish Cavaliers,' which, I am happy to say, are all very satisfactory indeed.

"I am, Gentlemen,

"Yours very truly,

"J. Noel Paton.'

"The Lays of the Holy Land" was projected by Mr. Watson, then the head of James Nisbet

37 Drummond Place
Edinburgh
April 27. 1879.

Sir,

I am sorry to find
myself again convicted
of culpable negligence,
in having left your last
beautiful proofs so long
unacknowledged. — As before,
excessive occupation, combined with indisposition is
my excuse. The blocks

May now be considered
quite satisfactory — and
sincerely wish there were
a dozen more of my drawing
in your hands.

With much thanks —

Very truly yours

J. Noël Paton

Mess.rs Dalziel

"On wheels of light, on wings of flame,
The glorious hosts of Zion came."

"The Song of Bethlehem."—CAMPBELL.

FROM "LAYS OF THE HOLY LAND."

BY J. R. CLAYTON.

By permission of Messrs. James Nisbet & Co.

and Co., who, mainly under our guidance, made a very wise selection for the figure subjects. Tenniel's are exceptionally fine, "The Destruction of Sennacherib" being perhaps the most important. The "Song of the Jewish Maiden," by F. R. Pickersgill, R.A., is one of his best, and there is a lovely drawing, "Ruth and Naomi," by J. H. Powell, but the one picture that stands alone is "The Finding of Moses by Pharaoh's Daughter," by Millais. The strength and power as well as the treatment are so original as to give it even in this fine collection a marked degree of undoubted prominence. Wolf has several exquisite examples, so has Birket Foster. Of our own drawings we will only mention "Tears for Jerusalem" and "The Raising of Lazarus." There is also a very beautiful drawing, "The Song of Bethlehem," in a fine decorative manner, by J. R. Clayton.

Clayton has been our friend and comrade for over fifty years. We met as fellow students at the Life School at Clipstone Street, when Edward Duncan was President and Treasurer, and Charles Keene, John Tenniel, George Boyce, H. T. Wells, and Arthur Lewis were amongst the regular workers.

This much-gifted, many-sided man began his artistic work as a sculptor with Sir Charles Barry, and under the influence of Sir Gilbert Scott, attaining much knowledge in architecture and ecclesiastical matters, he soon developed a decided taste for decorative work. During this period, however, his wonderful facility for design found an easy outlet in

THE FINDING OF MOSES BY PHARAOH'S DAUGHTER,

FROM "LAYS OF THE HOLY LAND."

BY SIR J. E. MILLAIS, P.R.A.

By permission of Messrs. James Nisbet & Co.

drawing on wood.   Our early connection with him
began on the *Illustrated London News*, for which
he did much beautiful work, notably some illustrations to " New Songs Written to Old Tunes,"
by Dr. Charles Mackay.   He also illustrated an
edition of " Krumacher's Fables," translated by
Dr. Hy. W. Dulcken, a dear old friend, who was
then one of the managers of Ingram and Cook's
book branch of the *Illustrated London News*.
Clayton also did a set of illustrations to " Bunyan's
Pilgrim's Progress."   We had the benefit of his
work in many of the " Fine Art Books " on which
we were from time to time engaged.   He did
the figure subjects for " Herbert's Poetical Works,"
and, in companionship with Sir John Tenniel, made
most of the figure subjects for " Pollock's Course
of Time."

Clayton's taste for decorative work gradually
took the form of stained glass, and his success in
that way became so extensive that the art of Book
Illustration sank into the background.   Although
not really one of the P.R.B., he was of them, and
with them in all their ways and works.   If the
Royal Academy had a more extensive scale of
fitness for the honour, there is no man to our
knowledge whose great ability as a true artist better
deserves the distinction of R.A.

Edward Duncan, George Dodgson and F. W.
Topham, with a few other members of the " Old
Society of Painters in Water Colours," formed
a club for outdoor sketching, the rule being that
at a selected spot all should sit down as close to

THERE'S NAE LUCK ABOUT THE HOUSE.
FROM "HOME AFFECTIONS WITH THE POETS."
BY SIR J. E. MILLAIS, P.R.A.

By permission of Messrs. George Routledge & Sons.

each other as possible, taking various points of
view according to individual taste. One day whilst
at work in a field on the banks of the Upper
Thames, they saw a sturdy farmer coming towards

Bowerswick Perth.
August 16. 57.

Dear Sir,

Both the illustrations
are so perfectly cut that I
have nothing to say, and therefore
will keep both the proofs, as
I should like to have them.
Perhaps you may just give down
one or two lines in the There was
luck in the upper line of the woman's
hand × ———— Run the shading of
the man's shoulder more into the outline.
also the little girls left leg × × had

the mans shoe and
run a little more decided light
down the Dogs nose 
Beyond these trivial corrections
I see nothing. I shall be
glad to see how the "Moses"
drawings cuts, these two are
most satisfactory

Yours very truly

John Everett Millais

Wᵐ Dalziel Brothers

them looking very fierce and angry. When he got near the party he said:

"What be you lot o' lazy devils a-doing in my field?"

"Sketching, sir, sketching!"

"Is that fit work for men? When the young ladies from Miss Gray's boarding school come down to 'sketch' I say let 'em; if it pleases them, it don't hurt me, an' there be no harm; but when I see a lot of great hulking men like you fellows about such nonsense it makes me fair angry! Why, domn it, you might be doing a lot o' good work o' some sort! I would rather break stones by the roadside for a shilling a day than fool away my time like you be doing. You ought to be ashamed o' yourselves, you ought!"

They tried to explain to him that they made their living by painting pictures. After some strong expressions of doubt the farmer sobered down a little and asked Dodgson how much he would get for the one he was "doing." Dodgson, knowing the sort of man he had to deal with, said:

"Perhaps as much as ten shillings, or maybe twenty if I can find a friend who fancies it."

The answer came, "Thee be a domned liar as well as a lazy lout!" Then with a look of contempt the tiller of the soil stumped away.

"The Poets of the Nineteenth Century," in addition to the two fine drawings by Millais already named, has many other good pictures; one of the most remarkable, perhaps, is the "Prisoner of Chillon," by Ford Madox Brown. Sir John Tenniel

"*From the window I look out,*
  To mark thy beautiful parade;
Stately marching in cap and coat,
  To some tune by fairies played."

"Threnody."—RALPH WALDO EMERSON.

FROM "HOME AFFECTIONS WITH THE POETS."

BY EDWARD DALZIEL.

By permission of Messrs. George Routledge & Sons.

is well represented, the "Death of Marmion" being one of his best. Sir John Gilbert, too, has several: "The Vicar," "To my Mother's Picture," and "Hohenlinden." So pleased were we with the latter design that we offered him a commission for a water colour drawing of the subject. His reply was, "Yes, and it shall be one of my best." And it certainly was one of his most successful as a highly-finished work and will always hold its own. There are also several interesting drawings by William Harvey, J. D. Harding, Edward Duncan, and G. Dodgson; a large number of exquisite examples of Birket Foster, and several figure subjects by J. R. Clayton, F. R. Pickersgill, R.A., Edward Corbould, and Harrison Weir. Of our own many drawings in this book we will mention a small roadside landscape, "Taste," and a single figure, "The History of a Life."

On February 6th, 1856, Mr. Ford Madox Brown, in returning a volume of the Illustrated Edition of "Longfellow's Poems," wrote :

"The bearer will return the volume of 'Longfellow,' which I have looked through with great delight; and I think it bears honourable testimony to the high excellence which wood engraving has attained in this country."

Subsequently, on seeing the volume, "The Poets of the Nineteenth Century," he wrote :

"Let me take this opportunity of expressing my admiration of the work you last brought out, and the drawings by Dalziel * in particular, which are most poetic and took us by surprise, although whether yours or your brother's I, as yet, know not. The Millais' are admirable, both as regards him and the engraver."

* The drawings here alluded to are by Thomas Dalziel, he having contributed about a dozen illustrations to the book.

"There, ye wise Saints, behold your Light, your Star—
Ye would be dupes and victims, and ye are."

THE VEILED PROPHET OF KHORASSAN.

FROM "LALLA ROOKH."

BY SIR JOHN TENNIEL.

In "Home Affections with the Poets," Millais
again stands pre-eminent in his two contributions.
"There's Nae Luck About the House," when
compared with his drawing of the "Finding of
Moses," is an apt illustration of his wonderful ver-

satility, and a proof that in art all subjects were equally within his power.

F. R. Pickersgill has some fine pictures in this book, his " Oriana " being full of tender feeling. Sir John Tenniel, too, is very strong, his " Fair Inez " being the best. Sir John Gilbert and Birket Foster are both very powerful ; the former in " When I Come Home," " The Two Angels," and " The Wee Thing " ; the latter in his " True Love," " Come Awa', Come Awa'," " My Sister Ellen," and " The Graves of the Household." There is a very clever drawing, " The Sailor's Journal," by George Thomas, and a grand picture, " The Shipwreck," by Edward Duncan. Among our own drawings in the collection are, " To Mary in Heaven," Emerson's " Threnody," and " My Mother Dear."

Among the first works of importance by Sir John Tenniel that came into our hands to engrave were several drawings for an illustrated edition of Tupper's " Proverbial Philosophy," as well as his contributions to the illustrated publications issued by the Art Union of London. He also made a great many important drawings for the numerous " Fine Art Books " which we produced ; among them we would particularly mention " Dramatic Poems," by Barry Cornwall, and " Pollock's Course of Time " ; likewise several exceptionally clever drawings for " The Ingoldsby Legends," published by Richard Bentley.

One of his most elaborate works was the set of illustrations to " Lalla Rookh." The drawings were all made on the wood with lead pencil, and were fine examples of his varied powers of design

"Poor maiden!" thought the youth, "if thou wert sent."

THE VEILED PROPHET OF KHORASSAN.

FROM "LALLA ROOKH."

BY SIR JOHN TENNIEL.

By permission of Messrs. Longman & Co.

and delicate manipulation—such as gave us great pleasure in the rendering. The book was published by Messrs. Longman & Co. If Tenniel had never done any other work than "Lalla Rookh," and those two remarkable books "Alice in Wonderland" and "Through the Looking Glass," they alone would have been sufficient to immortalise him. What a piece of work the frontispiece to the former is! What dignity and rare grotesque humour are shown in both these books! What beautiful pictures "Advice from Caterpillar' and "The Father William" make!—

and how perfectly they are all drawn! "Pig and Pepper," "The Kitchen Scene," and "Alice and the Duchess" are among the best.

As a matter of fact, Tenniel did not wish to do the second book, so Mr. Dodgson ("Lewis Carrol"), the author, asked various other artists to undertake the task, amongst them Sir J. Noel Paton, who, being out of health at the time, at once declined, saying, "*No*, Tenniel is the man." And most fortunately, both for author and artist, he was, the drawings being most grotesque, and the delightful fooling and outrageous fancy beyond description : for instance, "Looking - Glass House," "Tweedledum - tweedle - dee - dee," "Humpty-Dumpty," "The Lion and Unicorn," and last of all "Queen Alice." Such pictures were half the battle in the success of these two delightful little volumes.

During the process of completing the illustrations a great deal of correspondence, always of the most agreeable nature, took place with the Rev. Mr. Dodgson, as to their execution and finish. It is well known that he was more than usually critical, both with the drawings and with the engravings. Mr. Dodgson also entrusted us later with the drawings made by Mr. A. B. Frost — a very clever and highly esteemed American artist, who fully entered into the quaint humour of the text—for "Rhyme and Reason" and "A Tangled Tale."

So much was Tenniel engaged at this time that we always regarded his undertaking the pictures, seven in number, for our "Arabian Nights," as an act of kindness to ourselves.

ALICE IN WONDERLAND.
BY SIR JOHN TENNIEL.

By permission of Messrs. Macmillan & Co.

Outside his *Punch* work, we believe nearly all Tenniel's work for wood engraving was executed by us.

Messrs. Bradbury and Evans had at one time the idea of publishing an " Illustrated Shakespeare," and

10 Portsdown Road.
Jan.ʸ 11. 1870.

Dear Dalziel.

Are you disposed
to undertake the engraving
of another little book for
Mr Dodgson? — It is a
continuation of "Alice's
Adventures" and I am
going to work upon it at
once.

One line please to say
"yes"—and I'll let you
know the size of blocks &c.
In much haste—
Yours very Truly
J Tenniel.

All good wishes for the New Year!!!

THE SLEEPING GENIE AND THE LADY.

FROM "DALZIEL'S ARABIAN NIGHTS."

BY SIR JOHN TENNIEL.

By permission of Messrs. Ward, Lock & Co.

1

Tenniel was to do all the drawings, but beyond two very characteristic subjects which we engraved the project was abandoned. Doubtless he found the undertaking more than he could carry out when added to his weekly work for *Punch* and his other engagements.

No matter what other work he had in hand, he always contributed his weekly cartoon to *Punch*. The moral teaching of these drawings is beyond measure. Whether it be in caustic satire or exquisite pathos, he held the town for over fifty years, proving himself to be not only a great artist, but one who will rank amongst the highest of Britain's worthies.

Sir John Tenniel was never very effusive in his observations, though his remarks were invariably complimentary. The following are two of his letters received on submitting proofs for his correction :

"3 PORTSDOWN ROAD,
"*Tuesday*.

"DEAR SIRS,—The 'Falcon' proofs are everything I could wish. The third proof requires just a touch.

"I wish you would find me two subjects instead of those which I return herewith—something with more action or incident in them. I am quite tired of *love subjects*, they admit of so little variety of treatment.

"Before you send the wood for the 'Pollock'* drawings, I think it would be well for me to give you a notion of the size I shall require—whether half page, and so on—and this I will do when I have the book back again.

"I am, my dear Sirs,
"Very truly,
"JOHN TENNIEL."

---

* This refers to some drawings he had undertaken to do illustrating "Pollock's Course of Time," to be published by Messrs. Blackwood and Sons, Edinburgh.

THE CRAWLEY FAMILY.

FROM "THE FRAMLEY PARSONAGE."

BY SIR J. E. MILLAIS, P.R.A.

"3 Portsdown Road,
　"*Saturday.*

"Dear Sirs,—I like the proofs you sent very much, but they require just a little alteration, the ‘Rokby’* especially. I will touch upon them and return them to you.

"I have such an accumulation of work on hand just now that I do not feel justified in undertaking the two new subjects you have sent, as I do not know when I shall be able to let you have the drawings. I am doing some work for the Queen, and as it is wanted as soon as possible, all things else must wait till it is finished. But apart from this, the ‘Coronation’ subject, although a good one, is *very* painful. I should not like doing it on that account. And the other, although certainly very beautiful, I do not care much about illustrating just now—it requires too much thought to be disposed of hurriedly. I will, however, do my best to let you have the ‘Barry Cornwall’† soon.

"Yours, my dear Sirs,
　"Very truly,
　　"John Tenniel."

When the *Cornhill Magazine*, in 1859, was first advertised for publication at the price of one shilling, with Thackeray as editor, the announcement fell like a bomb in the midst of the magazine publishers — Blackwood, Frazer, Colburn, Bentley and others—for nothing of this description had even been so much as dreamt of before at a less price than the orthodox half-crown. The heavy government duty on paper, then only recently removed, may have been some apology for the high price hitherto charged for this class of literature, which at the present day is so far surpassed, if not

---

* An illustration to Sir Walter Scott's poem of "Rokby" to be published in "The Poets of the Nineteenth Century."

† Referring to drawings he was doing for an illustrated edition of "Poems by Barry Cornwall," published by Chapman and Hall.

LADY LUFTON AND THE DUKE OF OMNEUM.

FROM "THE FRAMLEY PARSONAGE."

BY SIR J. E. MILLAIS, P.R.A.

By permission of Messrs. Smith, Elder & Co.

always in quality certainly in quantity, at less than half the price of the great "Cornhill innovation."

In 1847 or '48 we were introduced to Mr. George Smith, of Smith, Elder and Co., and for several years executed a fair share of the engravings they required. Amongst the earlier of these works we contributed to "The Jar of Honey, from Mount Hybla," by Leigh Hunt, and "The Dwarf of the Golden River," by John Ruskin. During this period we were not infrequently brought into correspondence with Mr. Williams, literary adviser of the firm. He was a grand old gentleman, with a kind, sympathetic manner, which won for him the sincere regard of all with whom he became associated.

When the *Cornhill Magazine* was started we were asked by Mr. George Smith (whose courtesy and kindness were at all times most marked during the many years of our connection) to undertake the engravings, as he purposed issuing one or two full page plates with each monthly number. This we did for several years, producing during the time, among the more important works, charming illustrations by Millais, Richard Doyle, Lord Leighton, P.R.A., F. Sandys, and other artists, all of whom, as time rolled on, acquired a prominent position in their art.

Artists not being proverbial for the just appreciation of punctuality, many of these engravings were produced under great pressure, as the following letter from Mr. George Smith will show:

"DEAR SIRS,—I am delighted with Mr. Millais' drawing, and I am obliged to you for having engraved it so well

TEMPTATION.—HORACE SALTOUN.

FROM THE "CORNHILL MAGAZINE."

BY SIR J. E. MILLAIS, P.R.A.

By permission of Messrs. Smith, Elder & Co.

considering the pressure of time. There will be another illustration for the June number and another for August; Mr. Millais already has the proofs of the chapters of 'Framley Parsonage' for June and August.

> "Believe me,
> "Yours faithfully,
> "G. SMITH.

"MESSRS. DALZIEL BROTHERS."

Richard Doyle's "Bird's-eye Views of Society," which first appeared in the *Cornhill*, were afterwards published in book form, and had a very considerable sale.

It was also through our connection with the *Cornhill Magazine* that we were introduced to George Augustus Sala, who was at that time contributing a series of papers and illustrating the articles himself. On our submitting proofs for his correction or approval, he wrote:

"MESSRS. DALZIEL.

"GENTLEMEN,—I have received proofs of engravings. You will permit me to thank you for the exquisitely artistic manner in which my rude scratchings on Wood have been rendered by your graver. 'The Group of Beggars,' 'The View of Genoa,' and the background under the Arcade are, to me, marvellous. My chief defect appears to be heaviness and blackness of touch, caused by painfully defective sight. I will, however, endeavour to remedy this by using a harder point, and trusting more to your tasteful interpretation, without overloading my shadows with cross-hatching. There are a dozen more drawings to come, but I wanted to see the proofs of the first instalment before commencing the second batch.

> "Believe me to be,
> "Gentlemen,
> "Your very obliged Servant,
> "GEORGE AUGT. SALA."

LADY WITH HOUNDS.

FROM "LONDON SOCIETY."

BY SIR J. E. MILLAIS, P.R.A.

By permission of Mr. James Hogg.

CHAPTER IV.

BIRKET FOSTER, R.W.S., ALEXANDER STRAHAN, SIR E. BURNE-JONES, JOHN D. WATSON, HOLMAN HUNT, FREDERICK SANDYS, HARRISON WEIR, J. WOLF, J. M. LAWLESS, TOM TAYLOR, LORD TENNYSON, SIR JOHN E. MILLAIS, THE EMPEROR NAPOLEON III.

BIRKET FOSTER was a genuine man; kind and generous to a degree in all the ways of life. He stands as one of England's most popular landscape draughtsmen, and as a painter in water colour of great distinction.

We first knew him as a little boy with round jacket and turn-down collar. Later he came to be apprenticed to Ebenezer Landells to learn the art of wood engraving; but in this he made literally no progress, and Landells considering that as a landscape draughtsman he might be more likely to take a foremost position, the youth's attention was turned to this branch of art with the most satisfactory results. His improvement was very rapid, and all that could be desired by his employer.

Shortly before the termination of his engagement with Landells he went for a holiday to Scotland, where, unfortunately, he had a very bad accident, breaking an arm and receiving other serious injuries, which for a long time quite incapacitated him for work. It was during his illness that the period of his indentures expired, but as soon as he was well enough to resume work he insisted on returning to his duties that he might make up the time that had been lost; and this he did without any request on Landells' part. On his return we well remember seeing him at work in a little top room in Birch Court, E.C. He was making small drawings of pots and pans, teapots, gridirons, and other such articles for an ironmonger's catalogue, and said, in the most cheerful manner, " It is right that I should return here and do this work ; it is good practice, and will enable me to draw all these sorts of things with some practical knowledge."

Our first personal business connection with Birket Foster was in 1851, when we commissioned him to make a set of eight illustrations to " Kirk White's Poetical Works " for Messrs. George Routledge and Co. After this he illustrated several small books in a similar manner for us, as well as becoming a constant and very liberal contributor to many of the " Fine Art Books " which we produced. Amongst these we may mention " Wordsworth's Poems," where his many tastefully selected views of the Cumberland and Westmoreland Lake scenery give such a charm to the book ; also " Odes and Sonnets," illustrated by a series of very beautiful landscapes which were printed in tints ; " Summer Time in the Country," etc. After hundreds of his drawings had passed through our hands we asked him to make a series of larger pictures, which were to be the best and most perfect work he could do, and they were, as far as possible, to be thoroughly representative subjects of rustic English scenery.

Foster most readily undertook the commission,

and was very anxious to commence working upon it, as the following letter shows :

"DEAR SIRS,—I shall be most glad to do the 50 drawings for £300, and the vignettes at your own price; I will do them for £50 if nothing is said about it. You must give me this week, as I've a good deal to get done, but next week you shall have some 'Minstrels.' *

"Yours truly,

"BIRKET FOSTER."

Notwithstanding this, having regard to his other engagements and the elaborate nature of the drawings, he made but slow progress, and fully four years elapsed from the commencement to the completion of the work. During this time he had been elected a member of the Royal Society of Painters in Water Colours, and from the day he exhibited his first picture there, there was an ever-increasing demand for examples from his brush, and a corresponding delay in his completing this commission. It is somewhat interesting to state that the last drawing of this series was the very last he made in black and white for the wood-engraver's purpose.

Instead of the fifty principal subjects and the fifty small vignettes contracted for, at his earnest request we consented to reduce the fifty large pictures to thirty, and forego altogether the fifty small vignettes.

When the thirty drawings were completed we asked him to reproduce the entire series as water colour drawings, of such varied dimensions as he

---

* This alludes to some drawings he was making for an illustrated edition of "Beatie's Minstrel."

"_Come awa, come awa,_
An' o'er the march wi' me, lassie:
Leave your Southron wooers a',
My winsome bride to be, lassie.
Lands nor gear I proffer you,
Nor gauds to busk ye fine, lassie,
But I've a heart that's leal an' true,
And a' that heart is thine, lassie."

"Come Awa, Come Awa."—Thomas Pringle.

FROM "HOME AFFECTIONS WITH THE POETS."

By Birket Foster, R.W.S.

By permission of Messrs. George Routledge & Sons.

himself might decide, for which we offered to pay him the sum of £3000 ; but after giving the matter very careful consideration, he said, in consequence of his other engagements, he felt reluctantly compelled to decline the commission.

There is no need for us to dilate on the earnest manner in which Foster carried out these thirty subjects. He gave us such beautiful drawings, so exquisitely manipulated, that we naturally bestowed infinite care in their reproduction, and it was throughout a labour of pleasure and delight to us. We published the work through Messrs. Routledge and Co. as " Birket Foster's Pictures of English Landscape," and it is a satisfaction to us to be able to record that the book was fully appreciated by the British Public.

An important part of our scheme in preparing this book was to have a page of verse, either descriptive of or in sympathy with each picture, so that it might possess literary as well as pictorial interest. When our work was drawing to a completion, we submitted some of the proofs to Sir John Millais ; and it is, perhaps, hardly necessary to say that he was charmed with the pictures, and warmly entered into the idea of having poetic descriptions to them. When asked his opinion whether he thought Lord, then Mr., Tennyson would be likely to co-operate with us, he immediately, in the most generous manner, offered to write to him on the subject, saying :

"I wish I could give sufficient time to the subject, for to tell the truth there's nothing I should enjoy more than to do the verses myself. But, of course, my pictures place that idea entirely out of the question. But I'll tell you what I'll do," he continued, "I'll write to Tennyson and ask him to take the matter up—he's rather particular, you know, and perhaps he might the more readily consent to do it for me, than if you wrote to him."

The following letter from Lady Tennyson to Millais will show how the proposition was received:

"Farringford,
"*June 7, 1861.*

"Dear Mr. Millais,—Alfred was in the New Forest when your kind letter came, or it would have been answered yesterday, though I am sorry to have to answer the thing is impossible. Poems do not come to him so, and if they did not *come*, you are, I flatter myself, too much his friend to wish to find them there or anywhere.

"May I ask you to do him the favour to decline the offer as you will best know how to do with all courtesy.

"Accept Alfred's thanks for your kind invitation and for what you say about the portrait.

"Believe me,
"Yours truly,
"Emily Tennyson."

This letter was accompanied by the following note from Millais:

"My dear Dalziel,—I enclose Mrs. Tennyson's answer to my note. I said that not to bother him, if he couldn't say 'Yes,' to write himself. It is just what I expected; however, we have lost nothing by the attempt. I should have thought it easy enough to write a few lines to each, as I should find it easy enough to illustrate anything. I am sorry to have kept you so long for the two fellows seated on the gate.* Cut it with all your might.

"Yours very truly,
"J. E. Millais."

Ultimately the matter was placed in the hands of Tom Taylor, the dramatic author, who was at that

---

* This refers to a drawing for the *Cornhill Magazine.*

time art critic to the *Times*, as well as a liberal contributor to *Punch*, of which journal he subsequently became editor.   He wrote :

> "8 Richmond Terrace,
> "Whitehall, S.W.
> "*June 5.*

"Dear Sirs,—I have just received the proofs.   I have thought much over the subject of poems to Birket Foster's drawings, and I think that I would do what you wish on certain conditions.

"1st.—That I might call in aid my wife's verses, it being understood that she will do one here and there.   I may say that she is homely born and bred, and that her verses would be above the mark of my own, as far as I can judge.   She has written much, both words for music and music, before her marriage, as Miss Laura Barker, and her music is of a very high order.   I merely write this that you may understand I am not forcing a novice on you.   I wish her to be associated with me in the work, from a belief that the union of her with me will increase its value to the public.

"2nd.—The price I would suggest for thirty poems is £100. This is putting the work at 'Once A Week' terms, and is the lowest price at which I could write and do justice to both you and myself. If these terms suit you, I believe I could have the thirty by the end of July, or if your arrangement is to publish in parts, at the rate of four a week, the mode of payment to depend on that of delivery, *i.e.*, according as it is of the whole at once or of the poems in fours. I will retain the whole set of proofs till I have your answer.

> "And I am, dear Sirs,
> "Yours truly,

"Messrs. Dalziel.   "Tom Taylor.

"P.S.—I send you two samples of the kind of illustration I should supply to the drawings.

"P.S.—If my terms or my verses do not suit you, I should suggest your application to the Rev. J. W. Barnes, of Dorchester, author of two very remarkable volumes of poems in the Dorset dialect.   Our respective contributions to be distinguished by initials of the writers."

Taylor, in undertaking the commission, said :

"... Who played
Beneath the same green tree,
Whose voices mingled as they prayed
Around one parent knee!"

"The Graves of the Household."—MRS. HEMANS.

FROM "HOME AFFECTIONS WITH THE POETS."

BY BIRKET FOSTER, R.W.S.

By permission of Messrs. George Routledge & Sons.

K

"I accept this with great pleasure, for independent of the beauty of the work, Foster and I are both 'Tyne-siders,' and that will give an additional pleasure to me."

In August, 1881, we published an Édition de Luxe of the book, a large, handsome volume, the pictures all printed on India paper. On sending copies to Foster we received the following reply:

> "The Hill,
>> "Witley, Surrey,
>>> "*31 Augt., 1881.*

"My dear Dalziel,—Accept my best thanks for the three copies of the 'English Landscapes.' It is really a splendid volume, admirably printed, and the get-up is altogether charming.

"I sincerely hope it may prove a success.

> "With kind regards,
>> "Believe me,
>>> "Very sincerely yours,
>>>> "Birket Foster."

Wishing to present a copy of the book to the Emperor of the French, we wrote to his Secretary, and the following letter came as his reply:

"cabinet
    "de
"l'empereur.

"Palais des Tuileries,
    "*Le 19 Juillet, 1863.*

"Messieurs,—L'exemplaire des paysages anglais de Mr. Birket Foster que vous avez exprimé le désir de faire agréer à l'Empereur, est parvenu à sa haute destination. Mais Sa Majesté, presque toujours en voyage depuis, n'a pu encore examiner cet album qui, d'après ses ordres, doit etre remis sous les yeux à son retour à Paris.

> "Recevez, Messieurs, l'assurance de ma considération distinguée.
> "Pour le Sénateur, Secrétaire de l'Empereur,
> "Chef du Cabinet, et par autorisation,
>> "Le Sous-Chef

"Messieurs Dalziel."   "Sacaley.

"*I heard a thousand blended notes,*
While in a grove I sat reclin'd,
In that sweet mood when pleasant thoughts
Bring sad thoughts to the mind."

"Lines Written on Early Spring."—WORDSWORTH.

BY BIRKET FOSTER, R.W.S.

By permission of Messrs. George Routledge & Sons.

To which we replied expressing our wish that it should be a presentation work, when again the secretary wrote :

"CABINET
    "DE
"L'EMPEREUR.

"PALAIS DES TUILERIES,
    "*Le 6 Janvier, 1864.*

"MESSIEURS,—Avant de prendre une décision relativement à l'Album de gravures sur cois, d'après les paysages de Mr. Birket Foster que vous avez adressé à l'Empereur, Sa Majesté a exprimé le désir d'en connaître le prix. Veuillez bien faire parvenir ce renseignement au Cabinet.

"Recevez, Messieurs, l'assurance de ma considération distinguée.

"Pour le Sénateur, Secrétaire de l'Empereur,

"Chef du Cabinet, et par autorisation,

"Le Sous-Chef

"M.Mrs. DALZIEL FRÈRES."   "SACALEY.

"CABINET
    "DE
"L'EMPEREUR.

"PALAIS DES TUILERIES,
    "*Le 1er Février, 1864.*

"MESSIEURS,—L'Empereur a bien voulu accepter l'Album de gravures, d'après les dessins de Birket Foster, dont vous lui avez offert l'hommage. Sa Majesté a examiné ces planches avec intérêt, en a apprécié l'exécution et elle m'a chargé d'avoir l'honneur de vous adresser ses remerciments sincères.

"Recevez, Messieurs, l'assurance de ma considération distinguée.

"Pour le Sénateur, Secrétaire de l'Empereur.

"Chef du Cabinet, et par autorisation.

"Le Sous-Chef.

"SACALEY.

"M.Mrs. DALZIEL BROTHERS, EDITEURS."

The book was sent to St. Cloud, and doubtless perished in the flames when that picturesque Palace was burnt down during the Siege of Paris in 1871.

Lord Leighton in acknowledging the receipt of a copy of this book says :

"DEAR SIR,—When your messenger came yesterday I was unable to write and thank you and your brother, as I do now, for the very handsome present you have made me, of the extent of which I own I had not the slightest notion when I accepted it with so much alacrity the other day. I have looked through the volume with great interest, and am much struck with the great talent displayed in very many of the designs—some, I think, quite excellent—and with the great spirit and brilliancy of your rendering of them.

"Once more my best thanks.

"Yours ever faithfully,

"FRED. LEIGHTON."

Birket Foster was a constant visitor at our office in High Street, Camden Town, generally bringing a parcel of drawings with him. On one of these occasions the conversation turned upon water colour painting and the great demand there was for that class of art, when, having seen some of his slight sketches in colour, we expressed a little surprise that he did not "go in" for it. He replied that his wife had suggested the same thing, but—and he shrugged his broad shoulders, saying, "Um—I don't know—but we shall see—we shall see." He did "see," and all the art loving world knows with what result.

Foster's success as a water colour painter was quite phenomenal. There was a mad rush for his work by collectors, and the prices went up as a natural consequence. Down at Witley in Surrey, where he subsequently built a most charming residence, he said to us, "When I sit down in that chair after breakfast it means at least twenty guineas before I get up again."

It was about this time that two celebrated

picture dealers met at the Charing Cross Railway Station : they had taken tickets for Witley, and both knowing they had the same object in view, travelled down together. On arriving at their destination they found only one fly at the station. A. made a rush for it, when B. stopped him, saying, "No, sir; this is my fly. I telegraphed for it from London, but I will be most happy to give you a lift to Foster's ; only remember I am first." And he was "first," for he cleared out every scrap Foster had to dispose of, and A. had to go away empty handed.

On Foster's first visit to the Galleries after he had been elected a member of the "Old Water Colour," as it was then called, he was received in a most patronising manner by J. D. Harding, the then President of the Society, who complimented him, and dilated on the great advantage it would be to him being a member of the Society. He also begged him to appreciate this by a close study of nature, adding :

"If you do as I suggest, I have no doubt you will one day take a good place amongst the best of us."

It was Foster's invariable custom to make small water colour sketches for his more important black and white work ; sometimes they were partly pencil, or pen and ink tinted. Some little time before he seriously took to water colour painting, a West End publisher frequently asked him for some of these sketches ; so he gave his friend a "bundle" of original drawings, for which the publisher thanked him, saying that one day, when he could

"*The Earth herself is adorning*
This sweet May morning;
And the children are pulling on every side,
In a thousand valleys far and wide,
Fresh flowers."

"Intimations of Immortality."—WORDSWORTH.

BY BIRKET FOSTER, R.W.S.

afford to do so, he would have them bound in a nice book. It was after Foster won distinction as a painter that he said to us, "Those drawings would now represent a money value of some hundreds of pounds." His mother, a dear old Quaker Lady, who was present, said, "Thee mustn't mind that, Birket. Thee gave him the drawings and they are his, no matter what the value of them may be now."

Birket Foster naturally spent much of his time in the country, often locating himself at farm houses, and being of a genial nature always became very friendly with the people. On one occasion an old farmer took the greatest interest in the work as it went on, in fact to the extent that the old boy seemed to feel that he had a sort of partnership in the production of the picture. Some time after this a friend of Foster's, who stayed at the same farm, found the old man most anxious to know all about Foster, but particularly as to how much money he had got for the picture "that we done down here." The friend said, "A hundred pounds at least." The old man was incredulous, in fact he would *not* believe it. When assured that such an amount was small for a picture by so clever and popular a man, he seemed unable to grasp it, saying, "Why, it would be like pickin' up sovereigns as if they was turnips or eggs ; and if it was so, all I can say is, he must ha' sold it to a friend."

After the success of our volume Messrs. Routledge made a collection of engravings from Foster's drawings in their various books, for publication.

Here is an amusing letter from Foster on seeing this new work announced :

The Hill, Witley.
Surrey.

30ʳ June 1873

Dear Dalziel

I have just returned from Italy — and write at once to say there is no objection to Mess.ʳˢ Routledge sending me a cheque for 50 guineas or to the first Title Beauties of English Landscape — by B.F. On second thoughts I don't like Beauties — try some other word

yours &c

Mess.ʳˢ Dalziel   Birket Foster

When our book appeared the Press was unanimous in its praise. The *Times* said : " It would be difficult to do justice to these delineations of rural life and scenery without seeming to fall into extravagant praise " ; the *Academy* spoke of " the inherent beauty of the designs " ; the *Art Journal* of " the grace of composition and idyllic beauty " ; the *Saturday Review* of the " subtile feeling for rustic character, and his sympathy for the poor ; his curious love for unsophisticated company in sequestered places."

The public responded well, but not in large numbers—the days of large numbers had not then come.

But of all that was said about these pictures we most treasured a letter written to us by John Ruskin, which we regard as " an appreciation " from one of the best and most original writers on art matters of his period.

" GENEVA, *August* 12, '62.

" GENTLEMEN,—I am much obliged by your having sent me those beautiful Proofs. They are superb specimens of the kind of Landscape which you have rendered deservedly popular, and very charming in every respect. I wish, however, you would devote some of your wonderful powers of execution to engraving Landscape, which should be better than 'charming,' and which would educate the public taste as well as meet it. These pieces, however, are peculiarly good of their class—rich, gracefully composed, exquisite book illustrations, and very precious as examples of wood execution.

" Believe me, sincerely yours,

" MESSRS. DALZIEL."   " J. RUSKIN.

As the work progressed we sent proofs to Foster for approval or correction, and according to his custom he wrote all his remarks on the margin of the India

GRANDFATHER NURSING A SICK BOY.

FROM "GOOD WORDS."

BY JOHN PETTIE, R.A.

Published by Mr. Alexander Strahan.

paper.   These proofs were all preserved, and they show how completely he was satisfied with the care we had bestowed on the reproduction of his beautiful drawings.

It is a great pleasure to us to be able to state that these touched proofs are now the property of the Trustees of the British Museum, where doubtless they can be seen with John Ruskin's letter and some of Foster's own on application at the Print Room of that institute in Bloomsbury.

Birket Foster spent his latter years at Weybridge, where he died.   Surrounded by many old and sorrowing friends, he was laid to his rest at Witley, his beautiful Surrey home.

Having already engraved several drawings for *Good Words*, we were, early in the year 1862, asked by Mr. Alexander Strahan to undertake the engraving and entire control of the illustrations for this journal, which was being edited by Dr. Norman Macleod, a Scottish minister of great repute and a Chaplain to the Queen.   The offices were subsequently removed from Edinburgh to London, and shortly after the house added to its publications the *Sunday Magazine*, a journal devoted to "Sunday reading."   This was edited by another celebrated Scottish divine, Dr. Thomas Guthrie, author of "The City: Its Sins and Sorrows," and other works of a kindred description.   A great many of the illustrations for this periodical we also engraved.

This connection naturally enabled us to introduce works by the then most promising artists in black

Coach and Horses.

FROM "GOOD WORDS."

By A. Boyd Houghton, R.W.S.

Published by Mr. Alexander Strahan.

and white, and by many other men who have since taken a high position in art.

Alexander Strahan was the originator of the sixpenny illustrated magazine. His *Good Words*, considering the period of its advent, was equal to anything that has yet been done at that price, and, if measured by the distinguished artists and brilliant writers of whose work it was composed, it is a question whether any of the more recent magazines would equal it in actual merit.

Strahan is a man of great taste, both in literature and in art. We were indebted to him for introductions to a number of highly-gifted young Scotch artists. Amongst them were Orchardson, J. Pettie, MacWhirter, and Tom Graham, all of whom soon became famous and won honours of distinction. Pettie made several fine drawings for *Good Words*, and he and MacWhirter illustrated a beautiful little edition of Wordsworth's " Poems for Children," for which, by the way, Millais made a charming vignette. Strahan also introduced us to Robert Buchanan, who kindly helped us in some of our " Fine Art Books," concerning which we will speak later.

While engaged upon these publications it often happened that the drawings came into our hands so late that insufficient time was left for engraving. It might be that drawings came to us on a Saturday evening, and we were compelled to deliver the engraved blocks to the printers on the Monday morning. This could only be done by taking each wood-block into two, three, or four pieces, and by two, three, or four engravers working

KISS ME.

FROM "GOOD WORDS."

BY A. BOYD HOUGHTON, R.W.S.

Published by Mr. Alexander Strahan.

all the night through upon them ; for while any
strain might be put upon the engraver, no excuse
was permissible for keeping the printing machine
waiting for a single hour.   But under the circumstances, and by the best available means, we did our
utmost with the drawings that were placed in our
care for engraving purposes, though we are free to
admit not at all times with that success we ever
had so much at heart.

As examples of the many complimentary letters
we received from artists whose drawings we engraved
about this period, we may quote the following :

"New Place,
"Woodchurch Road, W.

"Dear Mr. Dalziel,—I consider the cutting of my drawing
quite a masterpiece, and in every respect up to my expectation.
There is nothing I can suggest that would improve it.

"With kind regards,
"Very truly yours,
"Seymour Lucas."

"Grove Lodge,
"Palace Garden Terrace, W.
"Messrs. Dalziel.

"Gentlemen,—I am *entirely* delighted with your rendering
of my drawing ; it could not be better done as far as work is
concerned.
"Yours faithfully,
"Geo. H. Boughton."

"Dear Sirs,—There are parts of it I like very much indeed ;
indeed I like it all, but some parts of it I think are perfectly
beautiful.
"Yours very truly,
"Richard Ansdell."

Our early friend, the late F. R. Pickersgill, R.A.,
frequently wrote in high appreciation of the careful

SIGURD.

FROM "GOOD WORDS."

BY SIR E. BURNE-JONES, BART.

Published by Mr. Alexander Strahan.

L

manner in which we had reproduced his drawings, but in deference to the wishes expressed by his family we refrain from publishing any of the letters.

When Mr. Alexander Strahan proposed that we should take the entire control of the art part of *Good Words,* we asked all our most distinguished artist friends to make drawings for the journal. Amongst others was Holman Hunt, who readily offered his co-operation, and also favoured us with the letter here given, which certainly foreshadowed the coming eminence of one who has made a lasting mark on the history of English art.

"*November 21st, 1861.*

"MY DEAR SIR,—I have looked over *Good Words,* and carefully read Miss Mulock's poem of 'Go and Come.' The poem I esteem very highly, and shall be pleased to do an illustration of some kind, although I cannot hope to do it justice in the little leisure I have between this and the time you mention as the date when the drawing ought to be ready.

"In addition to the desire to satisfy your anxiety with respect to the illustration to Miss Mulock's poem, I write to speak of a friend of mine who I feel very strongly might be of great value to you in the illustrating of *Good Words.* He is perhaps the most remarkable of all the younger men of the profession for talent, and will, undeniably, in a few years fill the high position in general public favour which at present he holds in the professional world. He has yet, I think, made but few if any drawings on wood, but he has had much practice in working with the point both with pencil and pen and ink on paper, and so would have no difficulty with the material. I have not seen him lately, but remember that he has sometimes said that he should like to try his hand at drawing on wood, so without further ceremony I will enclose a letter to him which you may use at your own discretion. His name, as you will see by the enclosed, is Edward Jones.

"Yours ever sincerely,

"W. HOLMAN HUNT."

SUMMER SNOW.

FROM "GOOD WORDS."

BY SIR E. BURNE-JONES, BART.

Published by Mr. Alexander Strahan.

Hunt's letter of introduction was followed by a
visit to Edward Jones (afterwards Sir Edward
Burne-Jones, Bart.,) at his studio in Bloomsbury.
The room was crowded with works of varied
kinds, in every sort of method, all showing wonderful power of design, vivid imagination, and
richness of colour. We were so fascinated with the
man and his art that we at once asked him to
paint a water colour drawing, size and subject to be
left to him. About that time he had painted a
picture, "A Harmony in Blue," for John Ruskin,
and it was suggested that ours should be "A
Harmony in Red." After some months the result
was a most highly elaborated water colour, "The
Annunciation." This, of course, was in his early
manner, and of great beauty. Later on he made
for us a Triptych illustrating the Birth of Christ, the
first subject being the "Shepherds Guided by the
Star," the centre the "Manger, and the third the
"Wise Men from the East." The work was fine
in conception and rich in colour. He also made
a set of small water colour drawings of the "Seven
Days," which were intended for reproduction in our
contemplated Illustrated Bible, for which he also
made a few drawings on the wood. His contributions to *Good Words* were very limited. At
our request, however, he made slight water colour
sketches from some of the few subjects he did do.

The two following letters show that at this time
he was quite unknown to the general public,
although he was appreciated in the highest degree
by those who knew him and his work:

WORLDLY WISEMAN.

FROM THE "PILGRIM'S PROGRESS."

BY J. D. WATSON, R.W.S.

By permission of Messrs. George Routledge & Sons.

"62 GT. RUSSELL ST.,
"*August 1st, 1863.*

"DEAR SIR,—Understanding that you are going abroad for a short time, I write to say that if agreeable to you I should like to keep 'The Annunciation' in my studio until you return; for, as I do not exhibit, that is my only way of letting people see what I have been doing. Pray do not take the trouble to answer if this will be convenient to you.

"And believe me, dear Sir,
"Very faithfully yours,
"E. BURNE-JONES."

"62 GT. RUSSELL ST.,
"*Oct. 17, 1863.*

"DEAR SIR,—Your messenger arrived an hour after I posted to you. I send the Triptych. You will have 'The Annunciation' next week; but until it is quite finished, I am unwilling to send it out of my studio. The little drawing of 'The Days' is at this moment gone to have a new glass put before it, but will be ready on Monday. I am sorry that it will not be before. In haste.

"Yours very faithfully,
"E. BURNE-JONES."

The following letter alludes to his election into the Royal Society of Painters in Water Colours, one of the three pictures necessary to be sent in being "The Annunciation." This gave him a place for public exhibition.

"62 GT. RUSSELL ST.,
"*Feb. 10, 1864.*

"DEAR SIR,—You may know by now that I was elected on Monday. The picture is in my studio again now; but if you will leave it with me for a week or two, I think I may find time before leaving town to do one or two things at it which I notice.

"Believe me,
"Very sincerely yours,
"E. BURNE-JONES."

His connection with the Society was of short duration, owing to an unfortunate incident connected

CRUSOE VISITS THE OLD CAPTAIN.

FROM "ROBINSON CRUSOE."

BY J. D. WATSON, R.W.S.

By permission of Messrs. George Routledge & Sons.

with an early exhibit of his. If we remember rightly, the picture was of a classic, semi-nude character, at which some "great lady" had felt very much shocked; in fact, to such an extent that she said it ought to be taken off the walls, as it was quite indecent. This the committee foolishly did, with the result that Burne-Jones at once resigned his membership—a course followed by his friend Sir F. W. Burton, at that time one of their most promi-nent members. It is only just to state that many years after, both men were urgently invited to return to the Society, and did so. But Burne-Jones never sent much of his work there, for fresh and larger fields had opened up to him at "The Grosvenor Gallery," followed by "The New," at both of which he was a great power. His work was always grand in subject, with the highest aim and noblest purpose. He was elected into the Royal Academy, but these other connections held him so close that he resigned his Associateship to make room for others to whom the honour would be of more importance.

The death of this highly gifted artist, who in himself combined all that is good, kindly, and generous, was universally regarded as a sad loss to the world of art.

Early in the Sixties we had been commissioned by Messrs. Routledge, Warne and Routledge to find an artist—"A new man, sir," as Mr. George Routledge expressed it, who could illustrate Bunyan's "Pilgrim's Progress" with a fair amount of origin-

ABJECT PRAYER.   BY J. D. WATSON, R.W.S.

FROM "LONDON SOCIETY."

By permission of Mr James Hogg.

ality, and give something better than had ever
been done in this way before.   This, we naturally
felt, was a very difficult task, and fully realised the
responsibility that would rest upon us for the success
or failure of the work — the number of artists of
great ability working in black and white at that
time was very different to what it is now.

We had had many conversations on the subject
as to the most fitting man for the work, when early
in the year 1865 Mr. Alexander Strahan sent us
two drawings to engrave for a short fairy tale he
was about to publish in *Good Words*.   There was
novelty and freshness of style, as well as a purity
of drawing, in the designs which attracted our attention, and at once suggested the idea that the artist
might be competent to undertake the pictures for
the " Bunyan."   On enquiry we found he was John
Dawson Watson, a young man living in Edinburgh,
who subsequently became eminent as a black and
white artist, as well as a painter in oil and
water colours, and a prominent member of the
Old Water Colour Society.   We at once wrote to
him about the " Pilgrim's Progress," asking if he
would send us two drawings as examples of the
manner in which he would propose to treat the
subject.   His reply came by return of post, not
accompanied by drawings, but saying he was coming
to London at once, and would call upon us on his
arrival.   This he did, and a very pleasant interview
terminated by our placing in his hands the commission to do one hundred drawings for this work.

It is perhaps hardly necessary here to state how

"*To seek the wanderer, forth himself doth come*
And take him in his arms, and bear him home.
So in this life, this grove of Ignorance,
As to my homeward I myself advance,
Sometimes aright, and sometimes wrong I go,
Sometimes my pace is speedy, sometimes slow."
"Life's Journey."—GEORGE WITHER.

FROM "ENGLISH SACRED POETRY."

BY FREDERICK SANDYS.

perfectly our confidence in J. D. Watson's ability was indorsed, not only by the publishers, but by the public voice and the pen of the critics ; this edition of Bunyan's immortal work being, in a pecuniary sense, among the most successful of the many Fine Art Books issued by the Messrs. Routledge. Immediately on the publication and instant success of this book, we were instructed to secure Watson's services in illustrating De Foe's "Robinson Crusoe" with a like number of pictures. This he readily undertook to do, and, as a series of drawings in black and white, they will certainly compare favourably with any work of the kind this country has produced.

After the "Pilgrim's Progress" and "Robinson Crusoe" perhaps there is no other work where the versatility of his power is so strongly shown as in "English Sacred Poetry," to which book he was a very large contributor, having no less than ten drawings to "Gray's Elegy in a Churchyard," and twenty or more to other poems—"Time and the Year," and "Scene in a Scottish Cottage" being among the best.

On one occasion Watson happened to be at our offices when Birket Foster came in. They had never met before, and on being introduced, seemed mutually pleased to make each other's acquaintance, and left together. This acquaintance ripened into a life-long friendship, Birket Foster marrying Watson's sister.

Watson was a kind-hearted, liberal-minded man, and gifted in many ways outside his art. In the

"'My father and my mother
   And my sisters four—
Their beds are made in swelling turf,
   Fronting the western door.'

"'Child, if thou speak to them,
   They will not answer thee;
They are deep down in the earth—
   Thy face they cannot see.'"
                    "The Little Mourner."—DEAN ALFORD.

FROM "ENGLISH SACRED POETRY."

BY FREDERICK SANDYS.

By permission of Messrs. George Routledge & Sons.

early days of our connection with him he often spoke of what he called his "fatal facility," and no doubt that gift told to his detriment. His art was no trouble to him ; and this was the root of a certain indolence shown in his later productions which, generally speaking, were far inferior to what might have been expected from his natural powers—though his work was at all times full of tender refinement, beauty and sympathetic feeling.

He did many very clever drawings for the periodicals. One of his finest, perhaps, was for *London Society*, the subject being the figure of a man on his knees in the attitude of "Abject Prayer."

During the sudden rage that sprung up for water colour drawings his work was much sought after by the dealers. We remember him on one occasion speaking of this eagerness for his pictures, and saying :

"I believe if I were to spit upon a piece of paper and smear it over with my hand they would declare it beautiful, and have a scramble who was to buy it."

On Watson coming to London our connection developed into close social friendship. We had a great liking for his work outside his black and white. The first picture we bought from him was off the walls of the Royal Academy, "A Pet Goat," a small but most highly finished work. He did several water colour portraits of members of our family, and some fine heads, by point work, in sepia-coloured inks. We also purchased several

CLEOPATRA.

FROM –THE "CORNHILL MAGAZINE."

BY FREDERICK SANDYS.

small water colour drawings from him which he made to be reproduced in colour.

Watson had great dramatic taste; his connection with Birket Foster, and the frequent visits to his big house, "The Hill," at Witley, in association with Fred Walker and two or three other kindred spirits, gave him plenty of opportunity for exercising his favourite hobby. In the plays they got up he was everything, leading business, scene painter, costumier, stage and general manager. He had a perfect knowledge of costume—used to cut out the dresses, and, with the assistance of his wife and sister, did all the "tailoring." These plays were delightful and a joy to all who had the good fortune to witness them.

"English Sacred Poetry" gave an opportunity for beautiful pictures, and in the work of the various artists engaged on it there seems to be a greater unity of feeling than is generally the case where the art is mixed. At the same time, perhaps there is no stronger contrast in method than that which exists between the works of Holman Hunt and Frederick Sandys: for instance, Holman Hunt's beautiful illustration to Dean Trench's pathetic verses, "The Lent Jewels" (which we made the frontispiece to the volume), and the two very powerful drawings, "Life's Journey" and "The Little Mourner," by Frederick Sandys.

Of the many high class drawings which appeared in the *Cornhill Magazine*, there is no one work more remarkable than that of "Cleopatra," by

"What question can be here?   Your own true heart
Must needs advise you of the only part;
That may be claimed again which was but lent,
And should be yielded with no discontent;
Nor surely can we find herein a wrong,
That it was left us to enjoy so long."

"The Lent Jewels."—RICHARD CHEVENING TRENCH.

FROM "ENGLISH SACRED POETRY."

BY HOLMAN HUNT.

By permission of Messrs. George Routledge & Sons.

Frederick Sandys, which for dignity and grandeur of design must always be regarded as a fine specimen of that artist's work.

Stacy Marks also gave us some of the best drawings he ever made for the wood engraver—notably "A Quiet Mind," "The Ring," and "The Two Weavers." From Harrison Weir we had a set of four drawings, "The Only One." Sir John Gilbert's "Landing of the Primrose" is a fine example, but not so good as his set of illustrations to "A Hymn." There is a grand picture of a storm at sea, "The Watching of Providence," by G. H. Andrews, and Charles Keene's illustration to "Contentment" is a very strong bit of work.

We engraved many of Keene's early drawings and were close friends, working together constantly at the Life Schools in Clipstone Street, next door to which he had his queer little box of a room, where for a long time he did all his work. It was a strange mass of scraps, sketches, studies; bits of costumes, armour, and "all sorts" of oddments in the way of properties. It was his custom to make several studies for each figure he drew, and many of them were pinned to the dilapidated paper on the walls, helping to make up the somewhat picturesque appearance of the place. We were very anxious to produce some large and important work with him, and offered him a commission to do an elaborately illustrated edition of "Don Quixote," one of the conditions being that he should visit Spain, with the view of collecting new material for the purpose. He liked the subject, and would have

"*There sits a lovely maiden,*
The ocean murmuring nigh,
She throws the hook and watches:
The fishes pass it by.

"*A ring with a red jewel*
Is sparkling on her hand;
Upon the hook she binds it,
And flings it from the land."

"A Northern Legend."—W. CULLEN BRYANT.

BY EDWARD DALZIEL.

Published by Messrs. D. Appleton & Co., New York.

undertaken it, but mainly on the ground that he could not bind himself to do any important work within a fixed time, he finally declined our offer. He felt that his best efforts were due to *Punch,* but even with the proprietors of that journal he objected to be put on any fixed agreement, like Tenniel, Leech, Du Maurier, and others ; for, he said, it would make him feel that he must produce a given amount of work in a given time. "No," he said, "I prefer to send in my drawings as I finish them, whatever they may be, and be paid for the work I have done."

We need hardly say it was a disappointment to us. This was before the "Don Quixote" of Gustave Doré had been given to the world ; and we fancy that Art is the poorer by Charles Keene not considering himself free to accept our commission.

Messrs. D. Appleton, of New York, requested us to provide a set of illustrations to the Poetical Works of William Cullen Bryant. They wished for a large number by Birket Foster, who at that time was at the very height of his popularity for black and white work. Out of something like one hundred pictures he gave us thirty-six, all of which are beautiful examples ; many of them exquisite little vignettes. William Harvey supplied some graceful pictures ; Sir John Tenniel, J. R. Clayton, and F. R. Pickersgill were responsible for several of the figure subjects ; while Edward Duncan drew some very delicate little sea pieces.

"Once this soft turf, this rivulet sands,
        Were trampled by a hurrying crowd,
    And fiery hearts, and armed hands,
        Encountered in the battle cloud.
            .   .   .   .
"Now all is calm, and fresh and still,
        Alone the chirp of flitting bird,
    And talk of children on the hill,
        And bell of wandering kine are heard."

"The Battle-field."—W. Cullen Bryant.

By Edward Dalziel.

Published by Messrs. D. Appleton & Co., New York.

There are many of our own drawings in this book, of which we make mention—" The Battlefield"; "An Indian Girl's Lament"; "Life"; "A Northern Legend"; "The Lady of Castle Windeck"; and "An Evening Reverie."

Harrison Weir sent us some good pictures of animals, notably "The Maiden's Sorrow." Weir, one of our earliest connections, is a gifted and brilliant conversationalist, brimful of anecdote—humorous and otherwise, a genial companion and an old friend.

He is a man of many parts : poet, painter, draughtsman, and naturalist ; and how much that word "naturalist" means in the knowledge that fitted him for the varied branches of art which he encompassed in his numerous works! Not the least amongst them being the many children's books he created.

One of the most beautiful books ever entrusted to our care, in which the pictures were to be by various artists, was the " Poems of William Wordsworth." We feel, when looking at the book now, after a lapse of forty years, how happy we were in having the co-operation of such very suitable artists as Birket Foster, Sir John Gilbert, and Joseph Wolf.

Wolf came of a family of agriculturists. Bred amid field, woodland and hedgerow, he gathered his love of all things beautiful, animate and inanimate, direct from Nature. From his earliest boyhood he had an intense love of birds, and so strong was his feeling in that direction that he never

"There, I think, on that lonely grave
    Violets spring, in the soft May shower,
There, in the Summer breezes, wave
    Crimson phlox and narcissus flower.

"There the turtles alight, and there
    Feeds with her fawn the timid doe:
There, when the Winter woods are bare,
    Walks the wolf on the crackling snow."

"The Maiden's Sorrow."—W. Cullen Bryant.

BY HARRISON WEIR.

Published by Messrs. D. Appleton & Co., New York.

lost a chance of dissecting and thoroughly making himself master of the anatomy of the specimen under his immediate observation. In maturer life it was not enough for him to give a surface resemblance to a bird; he was one of the earnest men who must go deep down to the very root of his subject. Whatever eminence he gained as an all-round naturalist, it is by his bird pictures that he will always stand out the more prominent.

As a book illustrator he became so popular that no collection of varied art seemed complete without one or more of his exquisitely graceful pictures.

He was a great lover of music, and would often dream away the idle hours, as he called them, on his favourite instrument, the zither; and *a propos*, surely there was much sweet and even grand music in his groups of birds, such as "The rooks sat high" and "The mother kite watching and guarding her nest."

In our long connection with the firm of Thomas Nelson & Sons, of Edinburgh, we made a large number of drawings and did much engraving for their books. The work was mostly of an instructive and amusing kind for young people. Among the various artists employed upon their publications, Keeley Halswell, who at that time resided in Edinburgh, did a great many drawings. The Messrs. Nelson had an art department in connection with their vast establishment. In this branch William Small was a pupil; and there he illustrated many of their story

"The careless words had scarcely
    Time from his lips to fall,
When the Lady of Castle Windeck
    Came round the ivy wall.

"He saw the glorious maiden
    In her snow-white drapery stand,
A bunch of keys at her girdle,
    The beaker high in her hand."
        "The Lady of Castle Windeck."—W. CULLEN BRYANT.

BY EDWARD DALZIEL.

Published by Messrs. D. Appleton & Co., New York.

books before he came to London to take a first place amongst the most distinguished artists in black and white. Small became an important contributor to the *Graphic* in its early days, and made many drawings for *Good Words* and other magazines of Strahan's. He also made a few clever drawings for Buchanan's "North Coast Poems."

We saw much of Mr. William Nelson, the eldest brother, during his visits to London, which were by no means infrequent. He was a man with a large, warm heart, and kindly, genial disposition, and though holding broad views in most matters, he (like the majority of his countrymen in the last generation) looked for many years with the greatest aversion on all things theatrical, and from his early training considered "the door of the theatre as the gate to destruction." At one of his quiet dinner parties Madame Antoinette Stirling and her husband were present, and the talk naturally turned on music and the drama, when he related the following as his first introduction to theatrical entertainments :

"On one occasion I was, very reluctantly, prevailed upon to go to the theatre to see the comic opera, *Les Cloches de Corneville.* At first I was indifferent to what was going on, but as the play progressed my interest increased so much that at the end I came away delighted at what I had seen, and the next morning, turning the matter over, I found myself none the worse, either bodily or mentally, for having been at the play. Indeed, the performance gave me so much pleasure, that I

"*In the mid-water, moving very slowly,*
With measured stroke of dripping oars, a boat
Appeared out of the fading mist of the morning."
"The Exiles of Oona."—Robert Buchanan.

By Thomas Dalziel.

By permission of Mr. John Hogg.

resolved to repeat the indulgence on every possible opportunity ; but that, of course, could not be done in Edinburgh. Feeling that I have lost a great deal of intellectual enjoyment, I make a point of going to a theatre on every disengaged evening I have when in London."

When James Hogg and Sons removed their publishing house from Edinburgh to London we became intimately connected with them. James, the father, was associated with many of Scotland's best and noblest writers : De Quincey was a friend and companion, also Professor Wilson (Christopher North), and Dr. Brown, the distinguished author of "Rab and his Friends."

The two clever sons, James and John, were both most resourceful men, full of energy and enterprise. James was one of the first to follow the example of the *Cornhill* by starting a Shilling Illustrated Magazine, *London Society*, which he successfully conducted for many years. He gave examples of Sir John Millais, P.R.A. ; Fred Walker, A.R.A. ; John Pettie, R.A. ; Tom Graham ; Gordon Thomson, and J. D. Watson. Amongst the lady artists were Florence and Adelaide Claxton, whose style of work well suited the nature of the publication. The Christmas Number of *London Society* held a prominent position for many years.

John Hogg, the younger brother, while publishing many books of a useful and instructive high-class character, also conducted the *Churchman's Family Magazine :* and when amongst the artists we

"*To seek their bread from public charity,*
They and their wives and children—happier far
Could they have lived as do the little birds
That peck along the hedges, or the kite
That makes its dwelling on the mountain rocks!"

"The Deserted Cottage."—WORDSWORTH.

BY JOSEPH WOLF.

By permission of Messrs. George Routledge & Sons.

find the names of Frederick Sandys, G. J. Pinwell,
and others, evidence of his capability for the position is afforded. John Hogg is an earnest Free-
mason, and closely identified with the publications
of the craft.

Nursery Rhymes! what delightful subjects they
give for pictures, and how often we have had the
pleasure of working on them. The first collection
we made is very fully illustrated by William
McConnell, "a comic artist" of some repute in his
day. He was the close friend of the Brothers
Brough and of George Augustus Sala, for whom
he made a set of elaborate drawings to illustrate
"Twice Round the Clock." McConnell was a
most prolific artist.

Our next essay on the same subject was a
commission from the Routledges, and was issued as
"Our Favourite Nursery Rhymes." This was altogether much more important from an art point,
many of the best draughtsmen of the time being
engaged upon it. J. B. Zwecker made a capital set
of drawings illustrating "Old Mother Hubbard";
while J. A. Pasquier, a very clever artist in black
and white, and a skilful painter in water colours,
contributed several appropriate designs.

We well remember presenting a copy of this
volume to Professor Sir Richard Owen, the great
naturalist. He said what enjoyment it had given
to him: it was like meeting the friends of his
childhood. The grand old man's face really beamed
with delight as he, in his sweet, quiet voice, said,

"*He swells his lifted chest and backward flings*
His bridling neck beneath his towering wings;
The female with a meeker charm succeeds,
And her brown little ones around her leads,
Nibbling the water-lilies as they pass."

"An Evening Walk."—WORDSWORTH.

BY JOSEPH WOLF.

By permission of Messrs. George Routledge & Sons.

"They have not only pleased me, but I will have
the further pleasure of showing all my young friends
these dear old Nursery Rhymes and Jingles"

In conjunction with Messrs. Novello, Ewer & Co.
we produced "Our National Nursery Rhymes."
The rhymes were set to music by J. W. Elliot,
and the pictures were of an important character,
A. B. Houghton, G. J. Pinwell, Stacy Marks and
others employed thereon being all at their best.
As well as many of our own drawings, there were
several landscape and rustic pictures by E. G.
Dalziel in the collection.

We produced the pictures for two other books
for the same firm : "The Sunlight of Song," being
a charming collection of sweet songs set to music,
and "Christmas Carols." Both were fully illustrated
by popular artists. Amongst those for the "Carols"
were many most refined and appropriate drawings
by Arthur Hughes, who was one of the most
earnest of the pre-Raphaelite Brotherhood, and who,
independent of his painting, did a large amount of
black and white work. We are doubtful whether he
made any drawings for "The Germ." Our first
connection with him was for "The Music Master,
and other Poems," by William Allingham, for which
he did two drawings ; one, a fairy moonlight subject,
being exquisitely beautiful. He did much fine work
for *Good Words*, and many fanciful fairy subjects for
Dr. George Macdonald's stories, which appeared in
Good Words for the Young, amongst which were
"On the Back of the North Wind" and "Chamber
Dramas."

CHAPTER V.

FREDERICK WALKER, A.R.A., R.W.S., CHARLES DICKENS, PROFESSOR HUBERT
VON HERKOMER, R.A., GEORGE J. PINWELL, R.W.S., A. B. HOUGHTON,
R.W.S., WARD & LOCK, FREDERICK BARNARD, JEAN INGELOW, ROBERT
BUCHANAN, J. M. LAWLESS.

FRED WALKER often said that he wanted to come
to us as a pupil, but that we would not have him.
When he left the North London Collegiate School,
where he was educated, he came to ask our advice
as to the method of drawing on wood, and as to
the chances of earning money as an illustrator. We
advised him to begin by copying, in pen and ink,
pictures from the *Illustrated London News* and
other illustrated periodicals, specially recommending
the works of John Gilbert and Birket Foster as
the best models for style and manner.

He then went to J. W. Whymper, who at that
time took pupils to learn the art of drawing on
wood. There he studied and copied the works
we had recommended, and so quickly acquired the
manner of John Gilbert that when he made designs,
so close was his imitation that his drawings might
easily have been taken for Gilbert's own work.
But his own individuality soon began to assert itself,
and he quickly developed into the great master he
was. During this period he occasionally came to
us for advice on various subjects, and we gave him
commissions on some boys' books for Routledge
and other publishers, including " Hard Times " and
" Reprinted Pieces," by Charles Dickens.

On sending Dickens a set of finished proofs

N

of the latter, we received the following letter in reply :

"FRIDAY, *Fourth October, 1861.*

"GENTLEMEN,—I beg to acknowledge the receipt of the India proofs you have had the kindness to send me, of the illustrations to ' Reprinted Pieces.' Both in conception and execution the illustrations are very satisfactory indeed.

"Faithfully yours,

"CHARLES DICKENS."

Walker made many drawings for *Good Words.* One struck us as being so exceedingly beautiful that we asked him to make us a water colour drawing from it, which he did ; and, apart from its being rather crude in colour, it is a charming work, called "A Dinner in the Fields"—a group of rustic children. This, we believe, was his first commission for a picture. His early paintings were not fine in colour. He did not evince much capacity in this direction until he went down to West Somerset, and worked side by side with his friend, J. W. North, whose influence, aided by the lovely colour of the district, brought about a marvellous improvement in both his tone and mode.

Walker was of a very excitable nature, and with his rapidly growing power and popularity, soon got a high sense of his own importance. One day he came to us in an angry, irritated state, saying he had just finished a large water colour drawing that a well-known dealer had promised to come and see, but had failed to do so. " I want, when he comes to-day, to be able to say, ' That picture is sold ' Can you help me in this humiliating

"God knows all he does for the poor baby; how cheerfully he carries him in his arms when he himself is weak and ill; how he feeds him when he himself is griped with want; how he folds his ragged jacket round him, lays his little worn face with a woman's tenderness upon his sun-burnt breast."

"The Long Voyage."—CHARLES DICKENS.

FROM "REPRINTED PIECES."

By Frederick Walker, A.R.A., R.W.S.

By permission of Messrs. Chapman & Hall.

position?" After a few words of consultation, we said, "Yes, we will give you a hundred guineas for it." The picture was not a good example either in subject or treatment. It was a social scene, called "Strange Faces," but had a special interest in the fact that William Harvey, whom we had introduced to Walker, stood as model for the principal figure.

His first picture in oil, exhibited in the Royal Academy, was done from his drawing, "A Woman in the Snow," published in *Good Words*, and engraved by us.

About this time we commissioned him to make thirty drawings on wood the same size as those of Birket Foster's "Pictures of English Landscape." These he willingly undertook, and worked at earnestly; but the great demand for his pictures increased so rapidly that the drawings came less and less frequently, and at last the scheme fell through, after his having given us some eight or ten. All of these were perfect works of their class, and it would have made a grand book had it been completed. Later, we published the engravings with those of other artists, mostly by G. J. Pinwell and J. W. North, first in "A Round of Days" and "Home Affections," and afterwards in an India paper edition, as "Pictures of English Rustic Life," by Frederick Walker, A.R.A., and G. J. Pinwell, R.W.S. One of the designs we had a small water colour drawing of, "Come in out of the Rain"; also one of "Strange Faces," which, being in his later manner, was far better than the original picture.

Of these rustic drawings, fortunately, through

"*In the midsummer holidays some of our fellows, who lived within walking distance, used to come back and climb the trees outside the playground wall on purpose to look at Old Cheeseman reading there by himself. He was always as mild as the tea—and that's pretty mild, I should hope! So when they whistled to him, he looked up and nodded; and when they said, 'Hello, Old Cheeseman! what have you had for dinner?' he said 'Boiled mutton.'*"

"The Schoolboy's Story." —CHARLES DICKENS.

FROM "REPRINTED PIECES."

BY FREDERICK WALKER, A.R.A., R.W.S.

By permission of Messrs. Chapman & Hall.

the aid of photography, several of the originals
were saved, some of which are at Kensington
Museum, where the beautiful manipulation of the
work may be studied—the material and method ;
the mixture of pencil, point work, in some instances
ink, and wash ; the delicate colour of the wood,
and the skilful use of body colour (Chinese white),
all combining to bring about a most beautiful result.

Walker had a fine sense of humour, which was
shown in the few drawings he did for *Punch.*

At a social gathering the commencement of a
new story by Miss Muloch was humorously discussed.
The opening chapter dwelt much on early childhood.
The term, " Sacred Blue Pinafore," being used frequently so tickled Walker's fancy that he there and
then made a rough sketch in blue chalk, which we
here reproduce. The same evening he made the
portrait sketch of his friend, W. P. Burton, a clever
but eccentric character, who was present at the
time.

Fred Walker's art culminated in the production
of his " Harbour of Refuge," one of the greatest
English pictures for beauty, pathos, and grandeur
ever painted. He said one day to a friend, " look
at that little old man sitting against the distant
tree : that is a portrait of myself when I get to be
as old as he."

We considered ourselves fortunate in securing
a few of his water colour paintings. Independent of those already referred to, we may mention
" Philip in Church," which was the first picture
that brought him into prominent notice, and has

A WOMAN IN THE SNOW.

FROM "GOOD WORDS."

BY FREDERICK WALKER, A.R.A., R.W.S.

Published by Mr. Alexander Strahan.

"O Sacred Blue Pinafore."

Sketch by Frederick Walker, A.R.A., R.W.S.

A Fancy Portrait Sketch of W. P. Burton.

By Frederick Walker, A.R.A., R.W.S.

always been considered a thoroughly representative work. It certainly helped to secure his election into the Old Water Colour Society.

3, St. Petersburgh Place
Bayswater.

Dec 22. 1863

Dear Mr Dalziel

Accept my apologies for not having before answered yours reply

The picture shall be yours & I am going at it hard as possible – Millais has just left me. much comforted both as to that & the photo. of your block, he made some suggestions however for Philip which will be an improvement –

You will I dare say be glad to ~~hear~~ hear (in confidence) that I intend becoming a candidate for the Old Water Color Soc? – chiefly on the advice &c of certain

*of its members, and should
like Philip as one specimen
This I particularly wish
kept snug at present—
Millais's advice is strongly
in its favor*

*I shall be glad to
hear from you. & perhaps
need not say that something
toward the plum-pudding
will gladen the heart of
Yours very sincerely
Fred. Walker*

E Dalziel Esq.

Years after, Professor von Herkomer produced a very charming etching of this picture, the same size as the original.

Gilbert Dalziel, son of Edward Dalziel, sat to Walker for the boy in " Philip in Church." Walker took a great fancy to him, and they had many games together. The following is a letter from

him to his youthful model, which will give an idea
of the nature of their friendship :

7 Charles St
Manchester Square
Feb. 11 1862

My dear Sur

I begg to enklose the
Top as i prom-missed and
1 or too Jew-Jabes which
You will kindley giv to youre
sister Miss Grace (with me
best compleymints) only on
the condilchion that She dont
gitt réd of em in less then
5 minites Hopping you are
wel as it leves me at preash-
unt I remain Dear Sur
Your es ~~~~~~~~~
Respketfuly
Fredk Walker.

G. Daljel Esquire.

For the first two years after the picture was finished it was seldom in our possession for more than a week or two at any one time, it being in frequent request, either for exhibition in the provinces or abroad; and not infrequently in Walker's own studio, when he wished to show it to his friends.

"Feby. 21, '66.

"MY DEAR MR. DALZIEL,—I have just received a letter from Miss Minnie Thackeray to say her sister, who comes to town to-day, is so unwell as to be unable to visit us to-day. Will you have the kindness to let the picture, which has just arrived, remain here for a day or two? and with many thanks,

"Believe me,
"Sincerely yours,

"GEORGE DALZIEL, ESQ."   "F. WALKER.

With reference to the following letter from Mr. Allen E. Everet, containing an application from the Birmingham Society of Artists that the picture might be exhibited at their rooms, we were given to understand that the Society awarded Walker their gold medal for the best water colour picture of the year. A like honour was bestowed by the Council of the Paris International Exhibition of 1865; in Dublin also, where it was on view, it was awarded a prize.*

"SOCIETY OF ARTS,
"BIRMINGHAM,
"2 July, 1864.

"DEAR SIR,—I just take the liberty of writing a line to ask if you have been able to obtain for us the loan of your fine

---

* It is a curious fact that on this occasion the picture was lost for some two or three months, but was ultimately restored to us uninjured.

drawing of 'Philip,' for our ensuing Exhibition, as all the members of this Society will feel most anxious to see this most interesting work on our walls this autumn? Hoping, therefore, that you will be able to oblige us,

"I remain, dear Sir,

" Respectfully yours,

"ALLEN E. EVERET,

"F. WALKER, ESQ." "*Hon. Secretary.*

Perhaps it is hardly necessary to say here that, with the exception of the first two, Walker made the entire series of illustrations to Thackeray's novel of "Philip; his way through the World," or that this picture is an elaborately finished painting from one of these designs. Walker held this gifted author in very high esteem.

In a note addressed to us, dated December 28th, 1863, we find the following passage:

"I have not been very well, and should have passed a happier Christmas but for this sad news of poor Thackeray. I have lost a good friend."

Our first knowledge of Professor Hubert von Herkomer, R.A., came to us in the form of a parcel, containing two or three drawings, through the post from Southampton. They were not very remarkable, but had sufficient skill to justify us in using his work. His development was wonderful, showing a facility of design and artistic taste far above the average. But in spite of his all-round cleverness he had severe struggles in the early days. He always had dramatic taste, and he told us that it was a chance whether he persisted in his painting or went on the stage.

He is a well-trained musician — a composer as well as an executant; and one time thought of joining a Christy's Minstrel troupe. In fact, he offered himself as "bones," but there was "no vacancy," so he continued drawing and painting, getting decorative work to do at South Kensington Museum, where he did some stencilling on a ceiling, under conditions explained in the following letter:

"32 SMITH STREET, CHELSEA,
"*Monday Morning.*

"MY DEAR SIRS,—Would you kindly send me the proof of my two drawings this week? I am working at Kensington Museum, doing some decorative work, which will at least keep the wolf from the door and still give, or rather leave, me plenty of time for other work.

"When I have some more things done I will take the liberty to show them to you.

"Yours very faithfully,
"HUBERT HERKOMER.

"P.S.—The zither still continues to be my dearest companion."

All this while he was gaining power, and whenever he had the good fortune to sell a picture he immediately "speculated" to the extent of going abroad for fresh study and experience.

The first picture of any importance that he exhibited in London was a large water colour— "Harvesters"—at the Dudley Gallery. It was a very clever work and fresh in style. We advised Mr. Strahan to buy it, which he did for forty pounds. Herkomer also made a full page drawing on wood from this picture for *Good Words.* On this success he went to Treport. It was at the time of the Franco-Prussian War; and here he painted a market scene called "Reading the News," which news was evidently adverse to the French. The groups of angry women and gloomy men tell the tale very clearly. When the people got to know he was of German origin, so great was their anger and hatred towards him that he was obliged to beat a speedy retreat for England ; but not before he had finished a very clever and characteristic picture, which, with the exception of the colour, holds its own with much of his later work. Upon this he was invited to join the Royal Institute, from which he retired, and later in life became a member of the Royal Water Colour Society.

We were fortunate enough to become the owners of the picture immediately on his return.

It was after one of his successful visits to Bavaria that he built a small wooden studio in the back garden of his house in Smith Street, Chelsea, and there painted, in 1875, his large oil picture, "The Last Muster," a production that will always rank as one of the finest English works. Soon after this he was elected an Associate, and in due course a full Member of the Royal Academy of Arts, as well as receiving several Continental decorations. Subsequently he succeeded John Ruskin as Professor of Painting at Christ College, Oxford. But all this is too well known to be dwelt upon here. Our own personal experience of Herkomer is that he is as good and generous as he is clever, and that whatever service we were able to render him in the past has been recognised by him over and over again.

"This is a sweet place, ain't it? a lovely spot? and I wonder if they'd give two poor, foot-sore travellers, like me and you, a drop of fresh water out of such a pretty, genteel crib? We'd take it wery kind on 'em, wouldn't us? wery kind, upon my word, us would."

"Tramps."—CHARLES DICKENS.

FROM "THE UNCOMMERCIAL TRAVELLER."

BY G. J. PINWELL, R.W.S.

"They looked like Time and his wife. There was but the one rake between them, and they both had hold of it in a pastorally-looking manner; and there was hay on the old woman's black bonnet, as if the old man had been playful."

"City Churchyards."—CHARLES DICKENS.

FROM "THE UNCOMMERCIAL TRAVELLER."

BY G. J. PINWELL, R.W.S.

By permission of Messrs. Chapman & Hall.

O

When G. J. Pinwell first called on us he brought a small water colour drawing with him. The subject was a lady of the " Old Ballad " style, with a decided sense of beauty in it, and in colour looked as if he had been studying the work of Holman Hunt. We recognised at once his cleverness, and that study and practice only were required to develop his great ability.

We first gave him some work on *Fun*, as is shown by this letter from him :

"DEAR SIR,—I now send you a *Fun* drawing, which I hope you will like.   I think it will print well.

"Believe me,
"Yours truly,

"G. J. PINWELL."

We also gave him, and obtained for him, work of the most varied kind, such as sets of illustrations for boys' books. He soon became a regular contributor to *Good Words*, and in its pages over one hundred of his drawings appeared. From several of them he painted water colour drawings, perhaps the most important being a highly finished work : "Landlord and Tenant," which shows his appreciation of character in the landlord, and of deep pathos in the fine group of the poor woman and her children. This picture was painted expressly for us and was never exhibited.

He made a few drawings for " Dalziel's Arabian Nights," but did not go far, as we had placed entirely in his hands our edition of "Goldsmith's Works," for which he made a wonderful set of

THE SISTERS.

PINWELL'S FIRST HIGHLY FINISHED PICTURE.

Reduced from an Engraving made for the "Graphic" by the Brothers Dalziel.

By permission of the Proprietors.

drawings considering the short time allowed for their production. He, however, lost nothing in force of design or in excellence, the manipulation only being a little less painstaking but more suitable for rendering in the reproductions.

Pinwell always objected to working against time: he held that if a thing was worth doing at all it must be done at his best. He often said that "money was not enough for him."

Amongst his most careful and finished work are the exquisite rustic pictures which we issued in "A Round of Days" and "Wayside Posies," also those to illustrate "Poems by Jean Ingelow," notably the sets for "The High Tide" and "Winstanly." He also did some strong character work for Robert Buchanan's "North Coast and Other Poems," some of a classic and romantic kind for his "Ballad Stories of the Affections," and a small set of illustrations to Charles Dickens' "Uncommercial Traveller." The pictures of "Old Time and His Wife," and "The Tramps," were amongst the best, and for these we gave him a commission to paint water colour drawings, and very exquisite examples they are.

When Pinwell was a little boy a lady asked his mother what she intended bringing him up to. She said she did not know, but that he was so fond of drawing she thought he would like to be an artist. "Oh," said the lady, "do not let him be that, for none but the best ever make any money." "But," said Mrs. Pinwell, "why may not my George be one of the best?" The dear old lady, of whom Pinwell

"*That's where it lies!   We get no good by asking questions, neighbour ;*
Parsons are sent to watch our souls while we are hard at labour.
This world needs help to get along, for men feed one another :
And what do we pay parsons for, if not to manage t'other?'
"An English Eclogue."—ROBERT BUCHANAN

BY G. J. PINWELL, R.W.S.

By permission of Mr. John Hogg.

always spoke with reverent affection, did not live
to see that he was "one of the best"—aye, of the
very best—of that wonderful group of young men
with whom he was associated ; for he possessed
some of the finest and highest qualities in a supreme
degree ; his sense of beauty, his fine colour, his
grace of design, his poetic art, being equalled only
by his force of character.   In much of his work
there is a tinge of sadness ; but as a rule, and in
his water colours particularly, beauty dominates
everything.

Outside our close connection with him as an
illustrator, our interest in him as a painter was
constant from the commencement up to the day of
his death—owning his first finished picture and his
last, on which he worked the day before he died.
His first he called "The Sisters"; his second, a
very highly finished picture, was "The Rats," from
"The Pied Piper of Hamelin."   While this was on
the easel we commissioned him for two others from
the same poem, "The Children," and "The Piper
Bargaining with the Burghers in the Market Place."
The latter was never done.   "The Children" we
lent to the Paris Art Exhibition, where it was
hung under a glass roof and "baked" until the
colour was all taken out of it, to the extent that he
said he would repaint it ; but after he had gone
so far with the *replica* he found it so hard a
task that he set to work on the first picture, the
modelling all being perfect, and restored the colour
to its original beauty.

One of the last pictures we purchased from

" 'Say it again,' cried little Jim ; and when,
  To please his heart, I said the song again,
  In through the smoky glass the setting sun
  Gleamed sickly ; and the day was nearly done."

"The Ballad Maker."—ROBERT BUCHANAN

BY G. J. PINWELL, R.W.S.

86 Adelaide. Rd

Dear Dalziel

I am very glad
You like the Old Clock
— and pleased that
it will go in such
good company
as to the money
I will take it as
I want it
Yours very
truly
S T Bunnell

£ 150

"Two young ladies, richly dressed, whom he introduced as women of very great distinction, and famous, from Town."

"The Vicar of Wakefield."

FROM "DALZIEL'S GOLDSMITH."

BY G. J. PINWELL, R.W.S.

By permission of Messrs. Ward & Lock.

Pinwell was "The Old Clock," it being a repeat of one of the rustic drawings he made for us.

At the time of his death we had acquired a great number of his finished works, both large and small. At the sale of the remainder of his works at Christie's we purchased about one third of the collection. Amongst them were two for which he had been commissioned by us—one, a repeat of "The Elixir of Love," smaller than the original, and, although unfinished, much the finer work of the two; the other a water colour repeat of an oil painting of "Vanity Fair," which he had in progress.

Two or three other unfinished efforts in oil, "The Earl of Quarter Deck," "Sally in Our Alley," and "The New Slipper," all go to show that he was a perfect master of the material; and had he lived to complete any of these, his election into the Academy would have been assured.

Pinwell had not the advantage of high culture early in life, but he was a true gentleman; though sometimes rough and brusque in manner, which showed most strongly when he came across or heard of any act of petty meanness, in all the ordinary ways of life he was good-natured, genial and sociable, brimful of tenderness, of a vivid imagination, and generous to a degree. His life was a truly domestic one, spending most of his time at home with a charming wife and a few chosen friends, amongst whom, perhaps, E. G. Dalziel and A. B. Houghton were the closest and most constant. He was the soul of good fellowship,

"*Whenever I approached a peasant's house towards nightfall, I played one of my most merry tunes, and this procured me not only a lodging, but substance for the next day.*"

"The Vicar of Wakefield."

FROM "DALZIEL'S GOLDSMITH."

BY G. J. PINWELL, R.W.S.

By permission of Messrs. Ward & Lock.

perfectly human, and sympathetic in the highest degree. Sir John Millais, speaking of him, summed him up in his own emphatic way, saying, "no man could produce work like his who was not a man of exquisite taste and refined poetic feeling."

"*Then, with a strange trouble in her eyes, Meg Blane Crept swiftly back into her hut again.*"

"Meg Blane."—ROBERT BUCHANAN

BY A. BOYD HOUGHTON, R.W.S.

Pinwell had all his life been in delicate health, and succumbed to a lung trouble at an early age.

A. Boyd Houghton was perhaps one of the most versatile of the black and white draughtsmen of our time. Amongst his early friends he was

"*And, ah! she trembled, fluttering and panting,*
While on my knees I fell."

'The Saint's Story."—ROBERT BUCHANAN.

BY A. BOYD HOUGHTON, R.W.S.

By permission of Mr. John Hogg.

called "The Young Genius," and his first efforts in art showed that he well deserved that appellation. He did not require the model set before him—to look at his subject was sufficient. It was like a "snap-shot" fixed on the brain, and memory was enough for his purpose. He had a vivid fancy, and was brimming over with the finest qualities of the designer's art. Our connection with him was a long and very close one. He was a most delightful companion—his fine sense of humour was coupled with a pleasant tinge of satire, such as comes from a man who knows the world in its various phases of life, but always cultured and refined.

One of his characteristics was his great love of children. It was a pleasure to him to get a party of young people together, and go off to the fields to romp and play all sorts of games and antics. His taste in that way is fully shown in the set of some thirty or more drawings he made for us of "Child Life," which we published, through Routledge, as "Home Thoughts." But he made other pictures of the little ones : "Kiss Me," done for *Good Words*, is an excellent example.

He had special advantages to assist him in his work on our edition of "The Arabian Nights." He was born in India. His father, his brothers, and many relatives were Indian army men, who had fine collections of articles of virtu, curios, costumes, and every sort of thing invaluable for the illustrator's purposes, much of which he placed at the disposal of Thomas Dalziel, thus enabling both to work with uniformity in all necessary details.

THE THREE BLIND MEN WATCHED BY THE THIEF.

FROM "DALZIEL'S ARABIAN NIGHTS."

BY A. BOYD HOUGHTON, R.W.S.

By permission of Messrs. Ward & Lock.

There is no doubt that these "Arabian Nights" drawings of Houghton's are amongst the best work in black and white of the period; but strange as it may appear, publishers did not take willingly to his art. Alexander Strahan was almost the only one who fully appreciated his great ability. He used his drawings largely in his various magazines and also bought several of his pictures—one, a large oil, "Sheik Hamel," a truly grand picture. We had a water colour of the same subject, which by many was considered the finer work of the two. Both were painted from the original drawing done for *Good Words.* One of the most beautiful water colours we had from him was "Coach and Horses," a portrait picture of his wife and two children, now in the possession of his youngest daughter, Mrs. Charles Davis, a lady of refined taste, whose greatest pleasure is to acquire works of her much-loved father. The small water colour of "Useless Mouths," exhibited in the R.W.S., was a subject he was very fond of—people being driven out of a beleaguered city. We had two oil pictures (which he painted with slight variations) of the same subject, as well as "The Daughter of Herodias Dances before Herod." Another, which he named "The Sorceress," was a beautiful young girl being tried as a witch before the tribunal of the Inquisition. Both the latter pictures were exceptionally fine.

We commissioned him for one hundred illustrations to "Don Quixote," which he did most ably. Frederick Warne & Co. published the book for us. His illustrations to "Krilof's Fables" are very

KING ZEYN CONDUCTS THE QUEEN-MOTHER TO THE VAULTS.

FROM "DALZIEL'S ARABIAN NIGHTS."

BY EDWARD DALZIEL.

By permission of Messrs. Ward & Lock.

P

clever.   He contributed to nearly all our "Fine Art Books," notably, "Jean Ingelow's Poems," "Our National Nursery Rhymes," "Buchanan's North Coast Poems," and "Ballad Stories of the Affections."

Houghton was the essence of kindness and generosity.   His impulsive nature knew no bounds. If any case of distress to a brother artist came before him he was the first to offer help.   We could give many special instances where he emptied his pockets that he might help those in immediate want.

Although we had done much work with the house of Ward & Lock from their first commencing business, it was not until 1863 that we held any financial interest in what they published.   In that year we entered into a contract with them to produce a series of popular standard works, fully illustrated, to be under the able editorship of Dr. H. W. Dulcken, and to be published with the general title of "Dalziel's Illustrated Edition."   We were to share equally in the cost of production, and participate equally in the profits, if there were any.   Before the first number appeared, Mr. J. Stephens, proprietor of the *Family Herald*, was so much attracted by the probable success of the scheme, that he begged to be included in the partnership, suggesting that all costs, losses, or profits should be equally borne by the three parties.   To this we agreed.

"The Arabian Nights' Entertainments," it was decided, should be the first of the series.   Some of the drawings were made by Sir John E. Millais, P.R.A., Sir John Tenniel, J. D. Watson, R.W.S.,

THE GENIE BRINGS THE HATCHET AND CORD.

FROM "DALZIEL'S ARABIAN NIGHTS."

BY THOMAS DALZIEL.

By permission of Messrs Ward & Lock.

G. J. Pinwell, R.W.S., and other artists, but the great majority of them were done by A. Boyd Houghton, R.W.S., and Thomas Dalziel.

This was followed by "The Works of Oliver Goldsmith," illustrated by George J. Pinwell, R.W.S. The work being entirely illustrated by one artist,

"Lord, hearken unto me,
Help all poor men at sea."
"Meg Blanc."—ROBERT BUCHANAN.

BY THOMAS DALZIEL.

By permission of Mr. John Hogg.

and he a very great one, gives it a special interest and value. Some of Pinwell's finest black and white is here seen.

Though these two books, upon which we bestowed much anxious care, were very highly

"And women barred their doors with bars of iron
In the silence of the night; and at the sunrise
Shivered behind the husbandmen afield."

"Celtic Myths."—ROBERT BUCHANAN.

BY THOMAS DALZIEL.

By permission of Mr. John Hogg.

appreciated by the press generally, and still more highly by the art-loving world, the public, unfortunately, did not respond so enthusiastically as we had expected, and, as a large debt had by this time been incurred, all further progress in the scheme was abandoned.

Amongst much interesting work in which we were associated with Ward & Lock, was a very charming edition of "The Pilgrim's Progress," containing 100 beautiful pictures, drawn entirely by Thomas Dalziel—thus adding another to the many editions of this wonderful book which we had been called upon to embellish.

Our connection with Messrs. Ward & Lock continued for many years after "The Arabian Nights" transaction had terminated.

It was through an introduction by G. J. Pinwell that we first met J. W. North. He began as a pupil of J. W. Whymper, in whose studio he made many small drawings, most of which were modelled on the works of Birket Foster. North said that all the art teaching he ever got at Whymper's was that when a subject was given him, a print of one of Foster's was placed before him, with instructions to make his drawing in that manner. We were struck, not only with the earnestness of his method, but the beautiful drawing and his sweet simplicity of style. But it is a fact that publishers generally did not care for his work, and, broadly speaking, all the drawings he did for us were in the form of commissions given direct by ourselves,

"*Silent they stood, each gazing on the dust*
Of kindred ;—on the well-beloved ones
Whom they should never lie beside in slumber."

"The Exiles of Glen Oona."— ROBERT BUCHANAN.

BY WILLIAM SMALL.

By permission of Mr. John Hogg.

and at our own risk. Most certainly we have
nothing to regret in this; for in different forms he
gave us some of the finest English landscapes that
have been produced in black and white. Amongst
the most important are those which we placed in
our "Round of Days," in "Home Thoughts," and
in "Jean Ingelow's Poems." And whatever reputation North may have gained in other branches of
art, we feel assured that these early works will form
no small part of that distinction.

From his earliest practice of art he devoted
much time to water colour painting, and was
elected, on his first "sending in," to the Royal
Water Colour Society, where he at once became
one of its most prominent members, producing, year
by year, landscapes of singular beauty. He also
painted several important landscapes in oil, which
called forth much attention at the Grosvenor and
at the New Gallery, and for some years now has
had the the distinction of A.R.A. as an affix to
his name.

It has always been a pleasant memory to us
in having had it in our power to be of some
service to this talented artist when he started on
"the battle of life."

We became possessed of several of his very
charming water colour drawings, one of the most
important being two beautiful rustic children looking
at a dead robin lying on the snow; another, "An
Old Wooden Bridge," the design of which he used in
illustrating one of Jean Ingelow's poems; and "A
Storm at Sea," which is an exquisite piece of colour,

"*Then calling to his henchman red,*
'Slit me the throat of the Priest,' he said;
'His red heart's blood shall flow before
A gracious sacrifice to Thor.'"

"Hahon."—ROBERT BUCHANAN.

BY EDWARD DALZIEL.

By permission of Mr. John Hogg.

Our first introduction to Jean Ingelow was through Mr. Niles, of Roberts Brothers, Boston, U.S., who wanted some illustrations done for her poems. Some six or eight page drawings were made by J. W. North, and the success of that venture induced us to make terms with her for the elaborately illustrated edition of " Jean Ingelow's Poems," for which we retained the English rights, and which we produced and placed in the hands of Messrs. Longman, her English publishers. The pictures were by various artists—Pinwell is at his very best in " The High Tide," " Winstanly," and many others ; so is J. W. North, who gave us numerous examples in his most refined manner. Wolf, Small, and Houghton are all there in good form. There is one fine example of Sir E. J. Poynter, P.R.A., of " Euphrosyne," and there are a number of our own drawings of which it is needless to particularize.

It was in our connection with *Good Words* that we first came in contact with Robert Buchanan, who was at that time coming right to the front as a popular poet. At our invitation he was induced to write and procure verses to the set of pictures by Fred Walker and others, which were published as " Wayside Posies," and for which he gave us much beautiful work. After this we made arrangements with him to produce an illustrated book, to be called " North Coast and Other Poems," which afforded plenty of scope for pictures of varied kinds. Commencing with " Meg Blane," a strong dramatic story of the sea is fully illustrated by A. B. Houghton

MUSIC.—A MAN AT THE SPINET.

FROM "GOOD WORDS."

BY J. M. LAWLESS.

Published by Mr. Alexander Strahan.

and Thomas Dalziel. "An English Eclogue" has a fine example of G. J. Pinwell; the same may be said of "The Battle of Drumlie Moor," and of the illustrations to "The Ballad Maker" and "Sigurd of Saxony." Houghton's pictures to "The Northern Warning" and to "The Saint's Story" are all powerful works. There are also two very fine drawings by William Small from the truly pathetic story of "The Exiles of Glen Oona."

"Ballad Stories of the Affections" was always a favourite book with us—the fine old ballads giving such an opportunity for pictures of an imaginative, poetic character. Two of Pinwell's—"Maid Mettelil" and "Young Axelvold"—are of exceeding beauty. Of A. B. Houghton's those for "Signelil, the Serving Maiden," and that for "The Two Sisters" are amongst his best. J. D. Watson has some good pictures, and those by J. Lawson illustrating "Aage and Elsie" are strong dramatic work. As to our own drawings, which are numerous, we will only say that we loved the subjects, and had much pleasure in making the drawings.

Among the many truly gifted young artists who came under our notice at this period was J. M. Lawless. His drawings were of such a refined and accomplished character that he at once took a place amongst the distinguished men of the time. He exhibited some few pictures at the Royal Academy which brought him prominently before the public; one of these, "A Midnight Mass," another, "A Sick Call"—a poor woman has been to fetch a priest, who, with his acolytes, is being rowed across a river; the woman's deep grief, and the solemnity of the entire scene, gives a touch of pathos to the group, and suggests it being a case *in extremis*. From "A Man at the Spinet," which we give, he painted a sweet water colour. Lawless was regarded as a "coming man," but, alas! like others of that "golden period" of Illustrative Art he passed away at quite an early age.

CHAPTER VI.

Lord Leighton, P.R.A., G. F. Watts, R.A., Sir E. J. Poynter, P.R.A. F. Madox Brown, Holman Hunt, Thomas Dalziel, S. Solomon. Sir E. Burne-Jones, Bart., F. R. Pickersgill, R.A., Sir George Grove.

"Dalziel's Bible Gallery" is composed of sixty-two pictures, most of which are of a very high order; many quite up to the standard we aimed at when planning our project for an "Illustrated Bible." Special mention may be made of those by Lord, then Sir Frederick, Leighton, Bart., P.R.A., whose drawing of "Cain and Abel" will always rank as one of the grandest examples of Biblical art of modern times; nor less highly must be estimated his "Death of the First Born." The "Samson" subjects also are very fine, particularly that of "Carrying the Gates"; and another notable subject is "Moses Viewing the Promised Land"; but all his contributions, nine in number, will stand amongst the finest of his works in black and white.

An art critic, in an appreciative notice of works exhibited at the Old Water Colour Galleries, where some of Lord Leighton's drawings were on view, wrote the following words in reference to one of the illustrations done for the "Bible" series:

"Whenever we have had anything to write of the late Lord Leighton we have always praised him as a draughtsman; we have always pointed to his book illustration as his greatest achievement. . . . "

"It is not, we must confess, so impressive a design as the grand 'Moses,' or the powerful 'Samson bearing away the Gates.' But it has been put together with all the dignity that the old decorators would have bestowed upon the subject, 'The Death of the

First Born.' It might have been, with its three panels beneath, designed for an altar. . . . The drawing was done for 'Dalziel's Bible,' a publication that was packed with as good book illustrations, as varied illustrations, as ever were produced in England, but that was financially a failure. There is, therefore, every reason why the public should never have appreciated the original designs. But though for Messrs. Dalziel the book was financially never a success, some day their effort to produce the best engravings they could from the best drawings they could get will be acknowledged."—*Daily Chronicle, Feb. 20th, 1897.*

The following letters will interest the reader, as showing how earnestly Lord Leighton entered into this project of illustrating the Bible:

"DEAR SIRS,—I have begun to consider the subjects you propose to me, and will shortly send you a list of the passages in the stories of Samson, of Elijah, and of Jezebel, which appear to me particularly to suggest illustrations. One question I would ask: when you spoke of 'six designs' was it that you wished no more from those chapters, or was it that some are already given for variety to other hands, or that you thought I would not do more for you? I ask this because the subjects I shall send you may be more likely twelve than six. By-the-by, eventually when you get to the Apocalypse I have a great fancy to design the Four Riders.

"I am, dear Sirs,

"Yours very faithfully,

"FRED. LEIGHTON."

Again:

"DEAR SIRS,—Many thanks for your letter. When I selected, as particularly congenial to me, the subjects from Elijah and those which concern Jezebel, it was only to secure them for myself eventually, as I have a great fancy for them, but I am quite ready to take the subjects of this year as early in the Bible as you please, if you will only send me your suggestions. Who is going to do that magnificent subject of the 'Promise to Abram that his seed shall be as the stars'? If no one, I shall be glad to take it. Of the three subjects you propose I should like to single out 'Moses Viewing the Promised Land' (not the design I made for St. Paul's) and 'David's Charge to Solomon,' also 'Balaam and his Ass' if you like. I don't see my way to

CAIN AND ABEL.

BY LORD LEIGHTON, P.R.A.

FROM "DALZIEL'S BIBLE GALLERY."

By permission of Messrs. Herbert Virtue & Co., Lld.

Dear Sir

I send the block
I promised you for the
end of this month.
— I need not say I trust
you will give peculiar
care to the modelling of
the flesh in which the slightest
deviation from the drawing
may destroy all anatomical
correctness — I should
wish the execution to be
facsimiled throughout
— nevertheless in passages
where the ink has clogged

and then shading become
spotty you will use your
discretion about clearing
the effects — in one or two
places also the lines will
perhaps require splitting
& make them grey —
the _white_ touches are of
course only corrections
— not high lights.

dr Sir

Yours faithfully

Fred Leighton

making a good thing of the 'Judgment.' The others seem to call for a great many figures, and you expressed a wish, when I saw you last, to confine yourself to subjects expressed with very few, if possible.

"The 'Samson' is indeed short, but contains much that lends itself for illustrations. I should have wished to treat the following subjects at least: 'The Angel Disappearing in a Flame after announcing to Manoah and his Wife, the Birth of Samson,' 'Samson and the Lions,' 'Samson and the Gates,' 'Samson in the Mill'; the other subjects from the wonderful story would require complicated groups. The above are all broad, simple, and very pictorial. As it is you will find it impossible to distribute your illustrations equally over a book like the Bible, in which one chapter will sometimes contain four or five subjects, and four or five chapters be without one. Will you let me know at your convenience what passages you would like me to treat *early* in the Bible this summer? It will save time if you can; I shall meanwhile ripen them in my head.

"I am, dear Sirs,

"Yours faithfully,

"FRED. LEIGHTON."

"*Monday.*

"DEAR SIRS,—Before starting for the Continent I write to tell you that you will, in a day or two, receive three wood cut drawings from me. I should have sent you a fourth which was also finished, and the best of the four (it represented the 'Escape of the Spies from the house of Rahab'); unfortunately at the last moment I spilt some indian ink on the upper part of it, and shall have a very tedious day's work to restore it, when I return early in November. I am sorry for this as I rather pleased myself on this design. I shall be in Venice all September—a letter addressed to me, *poste restante*, in that town, will find me. I start in a few hours.

"In haste,

"Yours faithfully,

"FRED. LEIGHTON."

Why Lord Leighton did not execute so many drawings for our " Bible " as he had originally intended, the following note will explain :

MOSES VIEWS THE PROMISED LAND.

BY LORD LEIGHTON, P.R.A.

FROM "DALZIEL'S BIBLE GALLERY."

By permission of Messrs. Herbert Virtue & Co., Ltd.

"DEAR SIRS,—I send you two designs for the 'Bible' with apologies for the delay in finishing them. I very much regret I find that the minute work—without which I cannot satisfy myself—on these drawings has proved terribly trying to my eyes. I must therefore ask you to relieve me, for some time at least, of my promises to make some other drawings, as I know that you have already suffered much delay. I hope you will not scruple to give away my subjects.

"In haste,
"I am, dear Sirs,
"Yours faithfully,
"F. LEIGHTON."

G. F. Watts, R.A., also expressed himself in high approval of the project, and promised his ready help, but ultimately he contributed only three drawings. His letter will be of interest:

"LITTLE HOLLAND HOUSE,
"*July 19th, 1863.*

"GENTLEMEN,—I am sorry my designs have been so long delayed. I have not succeeded in rendering one sufficiently satisfactory to myself to send to you. The fact is I have not the habit of making designs for wood cutting, and the subject is not a good one; my time also is fully occupied, and my health is not good. These reasons taken together may form some excuse for my apparent neglect; I don't think I can find time, anyhow, to make any fresh attempts for the next ten days or a fortnight, so perhaps I had better send you back the wood block. If you can wait till after that time I will again try what I can do, in order that you may not be disappointed, but I do not feel I can make much of the subject.

"Yours truly,
"G. F. WATTS."

Some slight objection having been taken to one of Mr. Watts' drawings, and a reconsideration suggested, he wrote the following letter:

ESAU MEETING JACOB
BY G. F. WATTS, R.A.
FROM "DALZIEL'S BIBLE GALLERY."

By permission of Herbert Virtue & Co., Ltd.

" December 16th, 1863.

" GENTLEMEN,—I am always ready to receive and act upon criticism, and have therefore added a little to the size of the head of Noah, according to your suggestion ; but my object is not to represent the phrenological characteristics of a mechanical genius, but the might and style of the inspired Patriarch. For the same reason I have thought it fit to give the length of limb and flexibility of joint still commonly seen in the East, tho' very rare in northern countries.

" I made drawing my principle study for a great many years, and consider myself at liberty to depart from mere correctness if necessary for my purpose ; especially if the incorrectness resulting be more apparent than real. The accompanying figure, traced from the drawing, as you can verify, will show that the disproportion is not much less than you imagined, and that the stretch of limb is perfectly possible ; at the same time I think it most probable that it would be objected to, and I do not ask you to risk condemnation, and by no means wish you to keep the drawing ; but if I do anything for you, or anybody else, I must carry out my own sentiment.

" I remain, Gentlemen,

" Yours very truly,

" G. F. WATTS."

Unstinted praise ought also to be given to the ten contributions of Sir E. J. Poynter, P.R.A. For conception of subject, beauty of design, and wonderful manipulation, they must all be regarded as fine examples of Scriptural art. We must specially mention the drawings from " The Life of Joseph ": " Joseph Distributing the Corn," " Pharaoh Honours Joseph," and " Joseph Presents his Father to Pharaoh." From the latter design he painted for us a most exquisite water colour drawing. Then, again, " Moses and Aaron before Pharaoh," " Miriam," and " Daniel's Prayer," are all remarkable for purity of treatment.

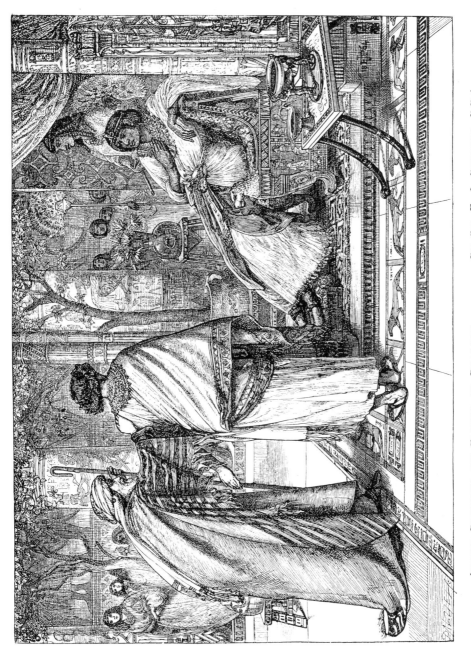

JOSEPH PRESENTS HIS FATHER TO PHARAOH.   BY SIR E. J. POYNTER, P.R.A.

FROM "DALZIEL'S BIBLE GALLERY."

By permission of Messrs. Herbert Virtue & Co. Ltd.

While arranging subjects for illustration for the
" Bible " we received the following note :

> "62 GREAT RUSSELL STREET,
>
> " *November 6th, 1865.*

"DEAR DALZIEL,—May I do the following subjects from the
Psalms ?—

"(1) 'David singing praises to the harp,' to be put either as
a heading to the Book of Psalms or to illustrate any of the Hymns
of Praise and Thanksgiving.

"(2) 'David penitent,' or a figure of ' Penitence,' to head the
Fifty-first Psalm. I have made sketches for these, which I think
will do. Something, I think, might be made of the following,
although I have no decided notion upon them as yet :

"(3) 'The Heavens declared,' etc.—*Psalm xix. 21.*

"(4) 'Yea though I walk through the valley of the shadow
of death I will fear no evil,' etc., etc., etc.—*Psalm xxiii. 4.*

"(5) 'The singers went before,' etc., etc., etc.—*Psalm lxviii. 25.*

"I dare say I could find more, but these are enough to go
on with for the present, no doubt ; if I think of others I will let
you know. I am sorry that you have again had to send in vain
for the ' Joseph' drawing, but the fault was not mine ; I was
out of town and had left word with the servant that she was
to give it to the messenger, which she failed to do. I think
I could go on with the two first subjects at once.

> "Very truly yours,
>
> "EDWARD J. POYNTER.

"I will take up your 'Joseph' drawing as soon as I can
manage to get up so far."

Sir E. J. Poynter, P.R.A., was born in Paris,
1836 ; and was educated at Westminster, Ipswich,
and Brighton College. He returned to Paris to
receive his art training, and entered the studio of
Gleyre, going afterwards to Antwerp, where he was
fellow-student with Alma-Tadema and George Du
Maurier. In Rome he made the acquaintance of
Leighton, and for a short time worked in his
studio there. He was elected into the Royal

MIRIAM.

BY SIR E. J. POYNTER, P.R.A.

FROM "DALZIEL'S BIBLE GALLERY."

By permission of Herbert Virtue & Co., Ltd.

Academy, 1869, and to full honours in that institution, 1876, attaining the highest honour, that of President, November, 1896. This is but a short record of a very brilliant career.

We were first attracted to his work, at a minor Exhibition in Newman Street, by a small, but very charming water colour drawing of " Egyptian Water Carriers "—two, half-length, beautiful girls—which we bought, on its merits, not having any previous knowledge of the artist. Several years after, this picture was engraved and included in our " Bible Gallery."

The following letter, remarking upon a proof from one of his drawings for the " Bible " submitted for correction, is one of several we received from Sir Edward J. Poynter during the progress of the work :

"UNIVERSITY COLLEGE,
" *Thursday, Nov. 28th, 1871.*

" DEAR MR. DALZIEL,—I have touched a little on the proof with a view to getting a little more breadth of light. The reduction so concentrates the effect that it looks rather spotty ; I was a little afraid it might. The light on the floor especially seems to want shading more gradually into the background ; cutting out the cross lines in the hatching on the left hand side would, I should think, do this, and thinning the lines generally as they get nearer the light. I have made a slight alteration in the head of the young lady standing up by taking out some of the shading, and one or two other points are touched with a view to simplicity. I hope I am not giving you too much trouble ! The engraving is most beautiful, especially the two near figures, which are wonderful ; indeed, whatever is wrong is my own fault.

"Very truly yours,
"EDWARD J. POYNTER."

We are tempted here to print a letter received from him in reply to one from us in congratulation

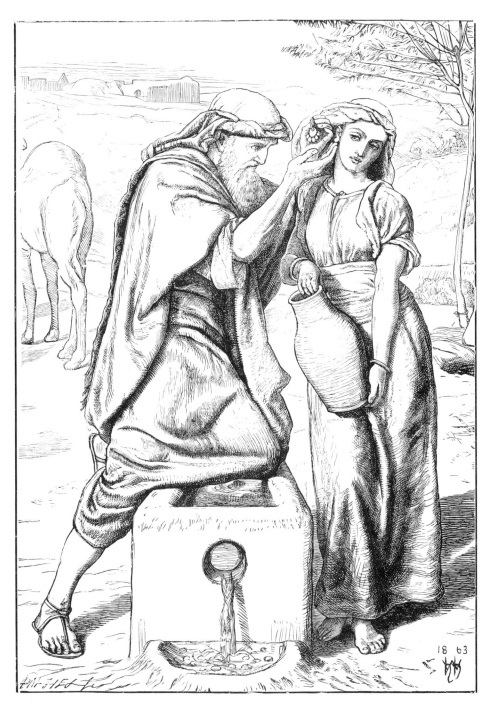

ELIEZER AND REBEKAH AT THE WELL.

BY HOLMAN HUNT.

FROM "DALZIEL'S BIBLE GALLERY."

upon his election as President of the Royal
Academy of Arts:

"28 ALBERT GATE, S.W.,
"*November 16th, 1896.*

"DEAR DALZIEL,—It was a very great pleasure to me to
receive your letter recalling the delightful times when I was
working for you, and the kind reception you always gave me
and my work. There is no part of my life or of the practice of
my part to which I look back with greater pleasure. Many and
cordial thanks for your friendly congratulations and good wishes.
I can hardly keep pace with my correspondence just now, or
these should have been sent earlier, for one of the first to welcome
me in my new and honourable post was your letter.

"Believe me,
"Very truly yours,
"EDWARD J. POYNTER."

The Holman Hunt drawing of "Eliezer and
Rebekah at the Well" is a work of such simplicity
of design and delicate treatment as might be expected from this distinguished artist, whose life has
been mainly devoted to Biblical art. Of the three
grand designs made for us by the veteran artist
G. F. Watts, R.A., we have selected that of "Esau
Meeting Jacob," as being a fine example of the
artist, who has always worked with the highest
and noblest aims. Of Ford Madox Brown's three
contributions we have chosen "Elijah and the
Widow's Son," as being not only an original conception of the subject, but perhaps one of the most
beautiful specimens of manipulative skill he ever
produced. He called it an etching, and so it was
to all intents, it being perfectly pure line work.
Although more beautiful, it is in no way finer
than "Joseph's Coat," or "The Death of Eglon."

ELIJAH AND THE WIDOW'S SON.

BY FORD MADOX BROWN.

FROM "DALZIEL'S BIBLE GALLERY."

By permission of Herbert Virtue & Co., Ltd.

F. Sandy's one drawing, "Jacob hears the Voice of the Lord," is a very strong piece of work. There are many other important pictures by F. R. Pickersgill, R.A., E. Armitage, R.A., A. B. Houghton, R.W.S., H. H. Armstead, R.A., A. Murch, William Small, E. F. Brewtnall, R.W.S., F. S. Walker, R.H.A., and Sir E. Burne-Jones. There are also twelve designs by Thomas Dalziel, which are regarded by many competent judges to be amongst the best work in the collection. "Hosannah," by S. Solomon, is also a very beautiful work. What joy and fervour of music are expressed in the drawing! We well remember the small picture he painted of the subject; it hung on the line at the R.A., and was looked upon as the work of a coming man.

Burne-Jones' "overwhelming" amount of work, as explained in the following letter, must be accepted as the reason why he contributed only one drawing to the "Bible," in which he took such keen interest at its commencement.

"52 GT. RUSSELL ST.,
"BLOOMSBURY,
"*Friday.*

"MY DEAR SIR.—In a few days you will have 'Ezekiel,' and soon after 'The Coming of the Dove to the Ark.' My work has simply overwhelmed me and my walks the last month, but for the fortnight I can almost give myself to your subject. Your private commission still delights me with its congenial nature. The three subjects you name explain the 'Noah' subject; as soon as I have made a scheme of the 'Carol' you shall have it, and consider about it. Do you think of having a 'Temptation of Adam and Eve'? It would be famous for engraving, with a horny snake all round the tree, and the naked figures could be sufficiently concealed in the thicket so as not to offend the prurient (for they ought not to offend the modest). I shall thoroughly enjoy all this

ABRAHAM PARTING WITH LOT.   BY THOMAS DALZIEL.

FROM "DALZIEL'S BIBLE GALLERY."

work. You may depend on having the 'Ezekiel' in a few days. I should like a larger block for 'The Building of the Ark.'

"Yours very sincerely,

"E. B. Jones."

Yet with all this vast array of talent our 'Bible," commercially speaking, was a dead failure. It was carefully printed on India paper, and issued partly in portfolio and partly in book form, but the British public did not respond, some two hundred copies being all that were sold. The balance of the number printed were disposed of at prices which we will not here record. Thus ended a work, begun with the highest aims, over which we spent many years of careful, patient labour, and several thousands of pounds.

Fortunately, many of the best of the original drawings have found their way to the National Collection at the Kensington Museum, where they will remain as records of some of the very finest examples of the black and white work of this period, and to the lasting fame of the artists.

It may be interesting to state that, at the time we were placing commissions for designs to illustrate the " Bible " and other important works in the hands of such artists as Sir F. Leighton, P.R.A., Sir John Millais, P.R.A., Sir E. J. Poynter, P.R.A., H. H. Armstead, R.A., A. Armitage, R.A., Sir E. Burne-Jones, A.R.A., Marcus Stone, R.A., John Pettie, R.A., W. Q. Orchardson, R.A., H. Stacey Marks, R.A., Professor H. Von Herkomer, R.A., G. F. Watts, R.A., Fred Walker, A.R.A., Fred Pickersgill, R.A., J. W. North, A.R.A., and

JACOB AND THE FLOCKS OF LABAN.   BY THOMAS DALZIEL.

FROM "DALZIEL'S BIBLE GALLERY."

By permission of Messrs. Herbert Virtue & Co., Ltd.

J. MacWhirter, R.A., all of whom have since attained the highest position in their art, without a single exception not one of them had at the time of our first correspondence entered into the ranks of the Royal Academy.

Almost the same may be said of many young artists who were not contributors to the " Bible Gallery," in whose hands we placed commissions long before they had risen to fame and fortune.

Frederick Sandys, on having a proof submitted to him for correction, wrote the following letter :

"MY DEAR SIRS,—The proof is absolutely splendid—one or two things I should like a little altered, but these I will see you about. I have two of 'Joseph' nearly ready, and have been for some month or more, but I have, unfortunately, crushed the bone of the top joint of the middle finger of my right hand. It is getting on well, and I have this week commenced working on a large picture, but I am debarred for the present still from touching the wood cut. I could not have sent the portrait of Mrs. Lewis to the Academy had it not been for some assistance kindly given me by Holman Hunt. I think I may promise, without disappointing you, one, if not two,* blocks in the first week in May.

"Ever yours truly,

"FREDERICK SANDYS."

Our original intention being to publish an " Illustrated Bible," we were desirous that it should be carefully watched through the press, and, if necessary, some few explanatory notes appended. With this object we offered the editorship to Sir George Grove. The following letter is of

---

* Notwithstanding this promise Sandys only made one drawing, " Joseph hearing the Voice of the Lord," for the " Bible."

HOSANNAH.   BY SIMEON SOLOMON.

FROM "DALZIEL'S BIBLE GALLERY."

By permission of Messrs. Herbert Virtue & Co., Ltd.

interest, explaining his reasons for declining the responsibility :

"CRYSTAL PALACE,
"SYDENHAM,
"*November 28th, 1863.*

"DEAR SIRS,—I have carefully considered the proposition you were kind enough to make to me and am reluctantly compelled to decline it. If I edit a Bible at all I should prefer it to be one in which the notes might bear a larger proportion to the text than that which you contemplate, and in which modification of the arrangement of the text itself might be introduced without imperilling the sale of the work, which they would no doubt do in the present case. And as I am not likely to be able to edit more than one Bible in my lifetime, I've no alternative but to reserve myself for a more favourable opportunity. I should also like to be more certain than I am in the present case that there would be no discrepancies between the illustrations and the notes. If you are not provided with any person to undertake the work I think I can recommend you a gentleman who would do it very efficiently. I am sorry that we will not have the pleasure of working together in this instance. With many thanks for your courtesy,

"I am, dear Sirs,
"Yours faithfully,
"GEORGE GROVE.

"Messrs. DALZIEL BROTHERS."

This refusal of Sir George Grove's co-operation, combined with other insurmountable difficulties which came in the way, caused us very reluctantly to abandon our *original project*.

Being invited to contribute to the Fine Art section of the Victorian Era Exhibition held at Earl's Court in the summer of 1897, we sent a frame containing selections from Tenniel's illustrations to "Through the Looking Glass," some specimens after F. Walker, and a large frame containing about twenty examples from "Dalziel's Bible," by Lord Leighton, Sir E. J. Poynter, Holman Hunt,

DANIEL'S PRAYER.

FROM "DALZIEL'S BIBLE GALLERY."

BY SIR E. J. POYNTER, P.R.A.

By permission of Messrs. Herbert Virtue & Co., Ltd.

Ford Madox Brown, Thomas Dalziel, Sir E. Burne-Jones, and others, with four proofs from Sir J. E. Millais' illustrations to "The Parables." For these contributions the Committee awarded us a Diploma for a Silver Medal.

Among our schemes for publishing high-class works was "The Biblical Life of Joseph," to be fully and carefully illustrated. We consulted Frederick Sandys upon the subject. The following letter will show the feeling with which he received the proposition :

"THORP, NEXT NORWICH,
"*Thursday, October 24th, 1861.*

"MY DEAR SIRS,—Many thanks, not only for my own proofs, but for those you were good enough to send Rose and Rossetti.

"I have not yet commenced the drawings of 'Joseph'—it requires an immense amount of research, and it would be most unwise to spoil the series, and I promise you the drawings as soon as you reasonably can ask for them. When would you like to have the 'Life' out—in twelve months? If so you shall have my drawings in time. I am coming to town in a week to make some drawings at the British Museum from the Marbles, and to get some Jewish dresses—can you help me here?

"I am doing all this that I may thoroughly, or, as far as it is my gift, make myself to be acquainted with Jews and Egyptians—to know all that is characteristic and beautiful, and avoid all that is hideous. Millais' 'Moses' is not a bit what I want—it is not a Princess ; a daughter of Pharaoh he has drawn. Now, what do you say about time? Let's have it out in twelve months. Autumn is the right time, is it not, for publishing? *

"With kindest regards to all of you.

"Believe me,
"Very faithfully yours,
"FRED SANDYS.

"The more I look at the cutting of 'Life's Journey' the more I am delighted and full of hope for 'Joseph.'"

---

* Unfortunately, Sandys never sent in one drawing for the book.

CHRISTIAN CLIMBING THE HILL OF DIFFICULTY.   BY E. G. DALZIEL.

FROM "BUNYAN'S PILGRIM'S PROGRESS."

Published by Mr. Alexander Strahan.

Of the many books placed in our hands for illustration, "The Pilgrim's Progress," by John Bunyan, exceeded in number all others. That immortal work came to us in every form—published at various prices, from one shilling, with a large number of original outline designs by a distinguished artist, to the edition produced by Alexander Strahan, in 1880, at five guineas. In this instance we printed all the larger pictures for him on India paper. There were one hundred drawings, no less than sixty-six of them being by that highly-gifted artist, Fred Barnard, whose dramatic power quite equalled his high sense of humour. Of his large pictures in the book, while all are good, those of "The Giant Despair," "The Man with the Muck Rake," and "The Atheist," are amongst the best. As to his smaller designs, it is difficult to say whether one admires them most for their strength of character or for the delicate and refined touch of his pencil.

There were other men of distinction to help Strahan with the full-page pictures. E. F. Brewtnall had ten drawings, all good. "The Three Shining Ones" is very refined and original in treatment. William Small's "Slough of Despond," and "At the Gate," are both worthy of this accomplished artist. E. G. Dalziel had five pictures, of which "Christian Climbing the Hill of Difficulty," and "Christian and Faithful Crossing the River of Death," are most remarkable works. John Ralston, another of the clever young Scotch artists who came to London, had three pictures,

OLD HONEST.   BY SIR JAMES D. LINTON, P.R.I.
FROM "BUNYAN'S PILGRIM'S PROGRESS."

Published by Mr. Alexander Strahan.

"The Ladies of the House—Beautiful Reading to Christian," being by far the finest. Sir James D. Linton, P.R.I., had four very powerful drawings, which were typical of all the work of this long-distinguished and painstaking artist, who always gives good sound readings of his subjects: "Old Honest" is an admirable example. Of Towneley Green's four pictures, "The Bundle Falls off Christian's Back," we like best; but all are good. The one picture by Joseph Wolf, "Lions in the Path," is simply grand.

A most important and comprehensive work which Messrs. Routledge entrusted to us was the production of the pictures for the "Illustrated Natural History," by the Rev. J. G. Wood. They were, of course, to be under the superintendence of the author, who was at that time Chaplain of St. Bartholomew's Hospital.

During the publication of the book, which was issued in monthly parts, and extended over a period of nearly four years, it was our custom to go there and see him every Monday morning, accompanied generally by Mr. George Routledge, to receive new lists of subjects, to report progress of those in hand, and to discuss the matter generally. From there we went on to the printing office of Richard Clay & Sons, who were printing the work under our supervision.

Among the many distinguished artists engaged we would first mention William Harvey, of whom we have spoken elsewhere. He did not, however, make

THE ATHEIST.   BY FREDERICK BARNARD.

FROM "BUNYAN'S PILGRIM'S PROGRESS."

Published by Mr. Alexander Strahan.

many drawings, from the fact that J. G. Wood thought them too mannered and conventional ; the same objection was held by the author to Harrison Weir. Although this clever artist contributed considerably to certain sections of the book, J. G. Wood summed up his drawings in a few words : "Always picturesque, but never correct."

Joseph Wolf, a German by birth, made a large number of drawings for the work, and gave the author every satisfaction. By many it is held that his birds are more correct than those by any other draughtsman ; certainly his perfect manipulation gives them a beauty that cannot be excelled. There can be no doubt that his contributions are by far the best : take his lions, tigers, or his groups of monkeys and of birds—all denoting the artist of high culture. He was appointed Special Artist to the Zoological Society, and worked very much at their Gardens in Regent's Park and also at their Museum.

While we were preparing the first sheets for the press, a very fine specimen of the gorilla, preserved in spirits, most opportunely arrived at the Zoological Gardens, one of the first, we were informed, that had ever reached this country. Permission was obtained for Mr. Wolf to be present at the opening of the barrel which contained the defunct animal, so that he might have a better opportunity of making notes for his guidance in doing the drawing, one of the best in the entire book, than the indifferently stuffed specimen in the Museum afforded him. Wolf afterwards remarked

MONKEYS.   BY JOSEPH WOLF.

FROM "WOOD'S NATURAL HISTORY."

By permission of Messrs. George Routledge & Sons.

that opening the barrel and lifting the animal out
of the spirits was extremely interesting, but the
effluvia was sufficient to poison a regiment of
soldiers—whether he considered it a fact that soldiers
as a rule are less susceptible to the influence of
poisonous gases than other men, he did not take
the trouble to explain.

From J. B. Zwecker, who was also a German
by birth, we had considerable help.   He was a
highly-educated artist of the Dusseldorf School.
He painted in oil and water colour ; his work
always showed good drawing and design, but was
generally heavy in effect.   He made a large number
of drawings for the " Natural History " and for
other publications—his being a ready pencil.   He
was an accomplished athlete, a genial companion,
a kind-hearted man, and an enthusiastic son of the
" Fatherland."

Another of the many-sided artists with whom we
were connected in this work was W. S. Coleman.
On coming to London he called upon us and we
were of some service to him, we believe, in introducing him as a wood draughtsman.   Beyond his
art taste and knowledge, he had considerable skill
in a literary way, creating some small books of
his own—" A Book on Butterflies," and another on
" Birds' Eggs," being amongst the first and best.
The Rev. J. G. Wood always said he could rely
on Coleman doing his utmost, for when living
specimens could not be obtained he would take
any amount of trouble in searching for the most
reliable representation of the objects required.

We must have had hundreds of his drawings through our hands. He painted both in oil and water colour, his landscapes in the latter medium being always very sweet and tender in feeling. In fact, Coleman's work ranges from a careful drawing of a butterfly—as decoration for a Christmas card—to classic or nude figures full life size.

T. W. Wood, an artist, in no way related to the Rev. J. G. Wood, made many careful drawings for the book—principally of birds and butterflies. Though always technically correct, he was deficient in artistic treatment—in fact, a playful artist friend once dubbed him the " Wooden Wood."

The commission to prepare the pictures for " The Natural History of Man" was also placed in our hands by Messrs. Routledge, in the same manner as for the " Natural History," with this difference, that, with the exception of implements —warlike, domestic and otherwise, huts, etc., which were all copied from the best authorities by other hands, the entire set of drawings were done by one artist, J. B. Zwecker, who, having an excellent knowledge of the human figure, was well qualified for dealing with the Kaffir, Zulu and other South African tribes, of which the first portion of the " History" deals so exhaustively. Zwecker always received his lists and instructions direct from the author ; our portion being the engraving of the wood blocks and a general supervision of the printing.

CHAPTER VII.

EARLY in 1865 Mr. Edward Wylam became proprietor of the comic periodical *Fun*—at that time the only competitor of *Punch*—and was fortunate enough to secure Tom Hood as editor. On taking up the direction, Hood informed us that one of the stipulations he made with Wylam was that we should be solicited to undertake the engraving of all the drawings. At first we felt some hesitation in accepting the commission, thinking it might considerably interfere with very important works we were then engaged upon ; but ultimately satisfactory arrangements were concluded, and our relationship continued in the most amicable manner, without a break for six years. In 1870—Mr. Wylam wishing to devote his entire attention to the development of "Spratt's Dog Biscuits," the patent for which he had recently purchased—we became the sole proprietors of the publication, paying for the goodwill and copyright the sum of £6,000, Hood continuing editor until his death.

In 1869 Hood commenced the publication of "Tom Hood's Comic Annual," which at once secured

THE OLD YEAR AND THE NEW.

FUN CARTOON, 1867.

BY PAUL GRAY.

a large amount of public favour. The second issue more than covered the slight loss sustained on the first. While the third issue was in preparation we purchased from Hood the title, copyrights, and stock of all literary and artistic matter connected with it for the sum of £600.

Tom Hood was, as perhaps half the world knows, the only son of the celebrated wit and poet, Thomas Hood, the author of "The Song of the Shirt," "The Bridge of Sighs," "Eugene Aram," and many other poems of great beauty and purport.

Tom Hood, like his father, was somewhat of an artist, possessing considerable skill in caricature, and giving a comic "twist" to his sketches. Many of

THE CHOSEN CHAMPION.   BY FREDERICK BARNARD.

FUN CARTOON, 1869.

his drawings are scattered through the pages of *Fun.*
He invariably expressed himself well pleased with
the manner in which they were reproduced. The
following is only one of many letters we received
from him:

"I am delighted beyond measure with the blocks. I have
returned some of the proofs, which I have touched for alteration;
which, with scarcely an exception, however, arises from my mistake
and not from the engravers'.

"Ever yours faithfully,

"Tom Hood."

During the many years of our intimate association
with Tom Hood, we received hundreds of letters
and notes from his pen, but the following is the
first and only instance in which he signed his name
"Thos. Hood." After this, when he had resigned
his post at the War Office and sat down steadily
to literary work, he always studiously signed his
name "Tom," with the express object that his
name might not be confounded with that of his
father, or that he should be accused of "making
capital" out of his father's name and reputation.

"21 Montpelier Square,

"Brompton, S.W.

"Dear Sir,—I believe Mr. Routledge has (or is going to
do so) given you the illustrations of my book to engrave.

"I need not ask you to do me justice, for I know you will
do that; but as I am not a professional artist, but an amateur, I
fancy I may give you more trouble to understand me at times.

"There are one or two blocks that I wish particularly to call
your attention to as requiring facsimile engraving, they being
likenesses. Two drawn in pencil I wish you not to touch, as I
intend, when I come to see you (which I hope to do soon), to
put in initial letters, as I think the fun in them forced. I have

FUN OFFICE.
80 FLEET STREET E.C.

Friday.

My dear Mr Dalziel

With joy I'd resort

To dine with the Shandies at fair Hampton Court
On Saturday, were I not bound on that day
To navigate Thames in the opposite way
As one of the crew of the screw "Albert-Victor"
(A steamboat that knowing ones vow is a pictur.)
Which is bound for sweet Margate, the Nore light beyond,
Being chartered expressly by Spiers & Pond,

(This is Spiers and Pond
the bard continues)

To take down a party — and 'mongst others me —
To Explore their famous new Hall by the Sea.

(This is the Haul by the Sea
Again the bard urges on his wild career)

So I'm forced — though I'd much like to come if I could —
To decline your kind offer.

Yours truly
Tom Hood

E. Dalziel Esq

drawn a rude sketch of them on the other side. I can introduce
them thus : a 'W' on the board, and an 'O' on the flag.   At
present I am sorry to say I am too ill to come over, but I hope to
be on my legs again by the end of the week.

"I am at the War Office from 10 till 4.   Should I be able to
see you at 5 if I called ?

"I hope this will not be our first and last connection in this
line, but that it will be a case of 'cut and come again.'

> " Believe me,
>> " Yours truly,
>>> " THOS. HOOD."

All our transactions with Hood, which continued
for close upon ten years, were of the most friendly
and agreeable character, leaving behind delightful
remembrances of his truly social and sympathetic
nature.   The letter which we give in facsimile was
received in reply to an invitation to join us at an
"up-the-river" dinner party, where we promised he
should meet a few kindred spirits and spend a very
enjoyable day.

Unhappily, Tom Hood died too soon, after an
illness of some short duration, against which he fought
with great courage.   He worked with the assistance
of his friend Henry Sampson, to the last—taking
part in preparing the number of *Fun* that was published the day after his death, which took place at his
house, in Peckham Rye, on November 26th, 1874.

Subsequently his widow handed us the following
letter, with the remark that they were the last
lines he ever wrote :

"MY DEAR SIRS,—To the best of my ability, and to the
utmost of my power, I have served you loyally and honestly while
strength remained. If I have failed it has not been wilfully, and
when we have differed in opinion I have only done what I have

AN URBAN DELUSION.

Jones knew a thing too much for most people. "Nice bunch o' water-cresses, just fresh in," said his greengrocer. "Oh, ah!" said the knowing Jones; "*fresh*—oh, yes! after being brought all the way from the country! Not for me, thankee!" For the fact was that the knowing Jones was just off for a day or two in the country himself.

OLD FATHER TIME.   BY GORDON THOMSON.

A PORTION OF *FUN* CARTOON. 1871.

AN URBAN DELUSION—(continued.)

But it so happened that the same bunch of water-cress went down by the same train as Jones did, and alighted at the same rural station. "Ha!" said Jones, in a stroll down the country lanes, "now, here comes a fellow with a real fresh country bunch of water-cresses ; I will buy them and take them home to town with me the day after to-morrow. *That's the way to get the real fresh article!*"

BY J. F. SULLIVAN.   FROM *FUN.*

believed it right to do, or assert beyond mere matter of expediency.

"Sampson has long co-operated with me, and now so well understands the working of the paper that it has been of the greatest comfort and use to me to have, for the first time in my life, some one on whom I could entirely rely when I was disabled.

"A more disinterested and faithful friend man never had, and I am sure if you transfer the bauble from my hands to his you will have secured fidelity and ability of no unusual order, loyalty and discretion, zeal and determination. It is my dying wish that he might be my successor on *Fun*. Of course I only express this as simply a wish of

"Yours always,

"TOM HOOD."

Among the many men, with whom our connection with *Fun* and the "Comic Annual" brought us into close communication, who have steadily ascended the ladder of fame—some, alas! no longer with us,—mention ought to be made of Henry S. Leigh, author of "Carols of Cockayne," "Strains from the Strand," and other volumes of verse; a man possessed of rare wit and unquestionable genius, but, unfortunately, without one atom of application or appreciation of the value of time. On one occasion, when some change of contributors was contemplated, Hood wrote:

"As for Leigh, he is hopeless: when perpetual motion is patented, a machine might be invented to bring him to the scratch regularly, but—he is unluckily a 'genius.' You might give him a retaining salary that would ensure—his never doing a line."

Yet, notwithstanding his extreme dilatoriness, he was a thoroughly good fellow, and Hood was at all times only too glad to receive any contributions he cared to send, for they were certain to contain some quaint conceit and out of the way sentiment.

THAT OR NOTHING.   BY G. J. PINWELL, R.W.S.   FROM *FUN.*

Mrs. Vicar.—"Thomas, what has become of you lately? I haven't seen you at Church for several months."
Thomas.—"Noa, ye ain't. *But I haven't been nowheres else.*"

On Leigh being remonstrated with for non-delivery of promised copy, we received the following :

> " 35 STRAND,
> "*1st Feb., 1881.*
>
> "*To* MESSRS. DALZIEL BROTHERS,
>
> "You have treated me so kindly that I dared, a little blindly,
>   An ambition and a future to your care to recommend.
> He is timid, he is nervous, but may God above preserve us
>   If we cannot stretch a point or so to gratify a friend.
> I have sent you oft a lyric, either genial or satiric :
>   Some were bad, and some indifferent, and some were very good.
> So my errors don't be hard on, but beneficently pardon,
>   Were it only through the memory of dear old Tommy Hood."

Of W. S. Gilbert, of "Bab Ballads" and Comic Opera fame, it may not be generally known that all those "topsy-turvy" rhymes were published in *Fun :* though they were by no means the only work he did for the journal. For a considerable period he wrote a comic paraphrase upon the most popular play produced during the week, as well as an extremely clever series of papers called "People I Have Met." He also wrote several stories for the "Comic Annual." In his selected edition of "Fifty Bab Ballads" he gives the following account of how these happened to be published in *Fun* :

> "It may interest some to know that the first of the series, 'The Yarn of the *Nancy Bell*,' was originally offered to *Punch*, to which I was at that time an occasional contributor. It was, however, declined by the then editor on the ground that it was 'too Cannibalistic' for his readers' taste."

W. S. Gilbert, like many of his fellow workers on the staff of *Fun,* began life in the Civil Service,

To Even Money!   By E. G. Dalziel.   From *Fun*.

Teetotal Wife.—"Ah, when that 'evingly Sir Wilfrid 'as 'is way, 'e'll put that nasty beer down!"

Irreverent Brute.—"Hope he'll put it down to the price it used to was—thruppence a pot."

he having been for a short time in the Education
Office; but the "diurnal drudgery" was not congenial. His impetuous temperament would not brook
direction or control, as his most intimate friends
were not slow to discover. Immediately on his
fairly breaking away from the "ten to four slavery,"
the first thing he did was to buy a quire or more
of foolscap paper, a bundle of quill pens, and a few
pieces of boxwood. Thus armed, he commenced
to fire away with pen and pencil, for at that time
Gilbert contemplated turning his attention to art.
His connection with *Fun* began in his early days,
when he sent some of his "topsy-turvy" things to
Mr. Maclean, the first proprietor, who, detecting
the unquestionable merit, insisted upon their being
accepted and published.

Clement Scott, another early and very valued
writer on *Fun*, in a short sketch of his own career,
referring to Gilbert, says:

"He was courteously, as a contributor, invited to the weekly
Fun dinners, and I fear from what I have heard, that at the
outset the young writer was not very courteously treated by some
of those who afterwards recognised his great talent to the
utmost, and became his warmest friends and companions. Frank
Burnand, owing to his novel, 'Mokeanna,' was promoted to
Punch; Tom Robertson, the dramatist, whom I met at the
club on the *Fun* meetings every week of my life for half a
dozen years; Arthur Sketchley, with his 'Mrs. Brown'; and for
verse writers, the delightful Henry S. Leigh, Saville Clarke, and
your humble servant, who has been writing bad verses for over
thirty-five years."

So long as Hood lived, George Augustus Sala
was a constant contributor, as were Edmund Yates
and Arthur Sketchley; the latter gentleman's " Mrs.

CHELSEA HOSPITALITY, UNDER A CLOUD.   BY E. G. DALZIEL.   FROM *FUN*.

Pensioner (to Workman).—" Got e'er a bit o' baccy about ye ? "   *Workman.*—" No, mate '.—just smoking the last bit '!
Pensioner.—" Come off that there grass—*directly !* "

Brown at the Play," as well as a long series of "Mrs. Brown" papers, chiefly comments on the current events of the day, were all published in *Fun*, and had immense popularity.

Another prominent member of the staff was William Jeffrey Prowse, a journalist of great brilliancy and power, and a "leader writer" and constant contributor to the *Daily Telegraph*. His advent, under the *nom de plume* of "Nicholas," was announced by Hood in the following quaint terms:

> "With feelings of considerable pride we inform our readers that we have been enabled (at some expense) to secure the exclusive services of the celebrated 'Nicholas.' . . . 'Nicholas,' that friend of man, has benevolently consented to impart (for a certain weekly stipend) the experience of—well, let us say *middle* age to the generous ardour of youth: AND THIS IS HOW HE DOES IT."

But Jeffrey Prowse was something more than the ordinary journalist working to order; he was a poet of no mean power. Some of his productions in this way were published after his death at the end of a small volume of "Nicholas Notes," edited by his friend, Tom Hood. Among his best are "To Be, to Do, and to Suffer," a poem showing great ability; and one named "The City of Prague," of which the following are the first and last verses:

> "I dwelt in a city enchanted,
>   And lonely indeed was my lot;
> Two guineas a week, all I wanted,
>   'Twas certainly all that I got:
> Well, somehow I found it was plenty,
>   Perhaps you may find it the same,
> If—if you are just five-and-twenty
>   With industry, hope, and an aim.

PARK LANE.   BY E. F. BREWTNALL.   FROM *FUN*.

He.—"What a dreadful noise there is down there with those cabs and things! You can hardly hear yourself speak."
She.—"Yes; almost as bad as being at the opera, isn't it?"

Tho' the latitude's rather uncertain,
   And the longitude also is vague,
The persons I pity who know not the city:
   The beautiful City of Prague.

.   .   .   .

L'Envoi.

As for me I have come to an anchor,
   I have taken my watch out of pawn,
I keep an account with a banker,
   Which, at present, is *not* overdrawn;
Tho' my clothes may be none of the smartest
   The 'snip' has receipted the bill;
But the days I was poor and an artist
   Are the dearest of days to me still!
Tho' the latitude's rather uncertain,
   And the longitude also is vague,
The persons I pity who know not the city:
   The beautiful City of Prague."

Poor Prowse died at the early age of thirty-four. Hood, in a short memoir, says:

"Prowse, as a writer, was gifted with a great charm of style; with a fertile imagination he possessed a logical mind. The amount of work he has done is astonishing, writing often two or even three leaders a day; and yet amid this constant and fatiguing trial he found time to write poems and essays, papers for the magazines, the annuals, and for *Fun*."

We must not omit to mention Ashby Sterry as one of the staff, and a contributor to *Fun's* pages of much graceful verse. He is well known for his volume, "Lays of a Lazy Minstrel." Then, Charles H. Leland, who gained considerable reputation as the genial Dutchman, Hans Breitmann. This gentleman contributed very liberally to the "Comic Annual." He is one of the most affable and interesting men it has been our good fortune to be associated

A DRAP O' THE BEST.   BY WILLIAM SMALL.   FROM *FUN*.

First Hielan'man.—"She'll pe ta pest whusky I shall have tastit for efermore."
Second Hielan'man.—"So tit I, neither!"
Third Hielan'man.—"Neither tit I, too!"

with. He was full of entertaining anecdote, a true artist and no mean draughtsman — in appearance, a giant, in manner as simple as a child. On one occasion in America he asked a negro the name of a black man of rather fine physique and superior appearance, who was standing near.

"He Injun," replied the nigger; "he big Injun; he heap big Injun; he dam heap big Injun; he dam mighty great heap big Injun; HE JONES." Jones appeared to be the nigger's culminating pinnacle of greatness!

Godfrey Turner, one of the talented young men who, in the early days, did so much towards placing the *Daily Telegraph* in the high position which it attained among the London morning papers, worked very constantly upon *Fun*, as well as on the "Comic Annual." Poor fellow! a protracted illness, generally attributed to overwork, incapacitated him during the last two or three years of his life.

Dutton Cook's short stories appeared constantly in the "Annual"—among his very last work being one he wrote for that periodical. Nor must we omit to mention Leman Blanchard, who was the author of more Christmas pantomimes than can well be counted. He did this work for Drury Lane under F. B. Chatterton, and then Sir Augustus Harris, for many years, as well as for many of the Provincial theatres. The able and accomplished editor of *Sketch*, John Latey, also was one of our most-esteemed contributors.

Henry J. Byron did much good work for

Fun under Hood, but he retired from the staff on commencing a paper of his own, under the title of the *Comic News*, which unfortunately for the proprietor had but a short existence.

Frank Barrat, Manville Fenn, Austin Dobson, Byron Webber, Moy Thomas, H. C. Newton, and Christie Murray, are the names of others whose work frequently appeared in *Fun* and the " Comic Annual."

On the death of Tom Hood we complied with his dying request and placed the " Bauble " in the hands of Henry Sampson, who had been a constant fellow worker with Hood for some two or three years previous. One of the first things Sampson did was to introduce George R. Sims upon the staff. It is superfluous for us to comment upon Sims' great ability as a dramatist, a writer of short stories and sympathetic ballads, because the voices of the reading and the play-going world have already proclaimed their high appreciation of his genius. Suffice it to say that it was in the pages of *Fun* that he found his first opportunity of appearing in print.

In 1893 when *Fun* passed out of our hands, he alluded to us in the *Referee*, with which he had long been associated under the *nom de plume* of " Dagonet," in the following kind words :

"It was by writing a small 'Poem' in *Fun* that I first won a little journalistic recognition. It was called 'A Dumpty Captain.' . . . It was in November, of 1874, that I first joined the staff of *Fun* and made my bow to the British public as an anonymous journalist. Tom Hood had just been laid to rest. It was in those days that I commenced my life-long friendship with Henry Sampson, the new editor. Though for me it was a time of struggle,

I would give a good deal for the light heart with which I braved the slings and arrows in those dear old days."

Again, Sims writes :

"Although I left *Fun* in 1877, my association with the Brothers Dalziel was never severed, and right up to the last issue (October, 1893) I was a contributor to 'Hood's Comic Annual,' of which they were the proprietors and editors. I have nothing but pleasant memories of the cheery, generous-hearted brothers and their clever sons; and I am delighted to hear that this year the honoured name will still be on the front page of 'Hood's Annual,' for it is to appear as usual under the editorship of Mr. Charles Dalziel.* "

Later, in January, 1894, he kindly wrote in the same paper :

"For nearly half a century the firm of Dalziel Brothers carried on the business of newspaper proprietors and engravers with credit to themselves and advantage to the public, and they gathered around them the best of young men, many of whom have become shining lights in the world of art and letters. To those who had the honour and pleasure of working under them, their friendship and their hospitality were always freely extended, and I have nothing but pleasant memories of the days when I was allowed to be one of their working staff.

"The Brothers Dalziel paid me the first money I ever received for verse. Tom Hood, the editor of *Fun*, had gone to Paris for a holiday, and Henry Sampson edited the journal in his absence, and gave me half a column to fill, and I plunged into poetry at once; and when I left *Fun*, in 1876, the Brothers wrote me a charming letter, which I still possess. Though my connection with *Fun* ended then, I remained one of the contributors to 'Hood's Annual' until last year; and so our business relations continued uninterruptedly and pleasantly for nearly twenty years—yes, for quite twenty years, for it was in 1874 that I did my first work for them. Had there been no Dalziels there might have been no 'Dagonet.'"

So long as Sims continued on the staff he was at all times a most welcome contributor, and, with

---

* This is the fourth son of Edward Dalziel.

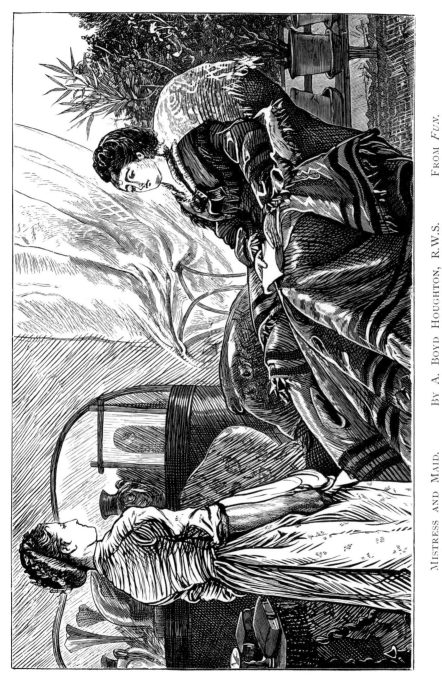

MISTRESS AND MAID.   BY A. BOYD HOUGHTON, R.W.S.   FROM *FUN*.

Mistress.—"Biddy, how is it you did not answer the bell when I rang?"
Maid.—"Sure, mem, 'twas bekase I didn't know what you was ringing for, mem!"

one exception, always to our entire satisfaction. The exception came about from the severity of a criticism which he wrote upon Sir Henry Irving's rendering of Macbeth, the humour of the article not being quite as apparent as it was intended to be. This caused Irving [and his friends] so much annoyance that he commenced an action against us for libel. However, Sims at once acknowledged the authorship of the article, with ample apologies and regrets, and assurance that there was no "malice aforethought," and Henry Sampson did the same as the responsible editor, so Sir Henry, in a very handsome and kindly manner, withdrew from the prosecution, and the matter ended.

For several years George Dalziel (the elder of the Brothers), regularly contributed short stories and verse to "Hood's Annual." Among the latter was a rather lengthy poem, of which we give a few of the verses :

WHAT THE MOON SAW.

Oh, can the earth, so dream-like sleeping lie
    Beneath the rays of that pale silvery moon,
That never gives a weary moan or cry,
    Or sign that sorrow dwelt 'twixt night and noon ?
There, calmly sailing on amid the stars,
    She looks as though no ruthless thought nor care,
Nor wicked deed could ever be that mars
    And lays the black spots of our nature bare.

She looks as though she never yet had seen
    An ill deed done in all the million years
That she has gazed upon the earth, or been
    Pale witness to a flood of bitter tears, —
Pale witness to the darkest deeds that man,
    With demon brooding in his heart, could frame :
Foul, miry spots her gentle eye doth scan,
    And "Lady Moon" goes smiling, all the same

Lo! she did see the budding earth when young:
  She saw the first red rose that e'er did bloom;
She heard the first grand carol that was sung,
  And saw the mountains clothed with golden broom.
She heard each silvery stream and gurgling brook
  Hymn its new song of never-ending praise,
And leaves and flowers, in every ferny nook,
  Sing psalms to greet the glorious king of days.

   .   .   .   .

She heard the first wild notes of Jubal's lyre,
  That fell upon the ear like magic sound—
The first bright spark of that celestial fire
  That thrills with rapture rare the whole world round.
She heard the first loud burst of ocean roar,
  And saw the crested waves careering fly;—
She heard its ripple kiss the sandy shore,—
  And saw the white foam dash against the sky.

   .   .   .   .

Years, centuries told, come on, and quickly fly,
  And this world rolls beneath the silvery moon
As she sails calmly through the deep blue sky
  Unheeding joy or sorrow, night or noon.
Unheeding revel, wail, or bitter cry,
  Or joy, or grief, or weary toil, or rest,—
She slowly climbs the ever-darkening sky,
  While dying sunlight pales upon her breast.

GEORGE DALZIEL.

From another issue of the "Annual" we make
a few extracts from some verses which are entitled:

MY BOOKS.

My books! my friends, my dear companions all!
  My never-failing—ever true and fair!
There standing round, come ready to my call,
  And talk, and sing, and tell their wonders rare.
If I am sad, they give me joyous song;
  Or if I wish for pleasant talk the while,
My friends are there, and will for short or long,
  Just as I please, the ling'ring hour beguile.

With them at ease I play the conjurer's part,—
    They bring for me the stores of other times, —
Oh, rare the grace !—oh, rare the cunning art
    That stirs the sluggish heart with ringing rhymes !

I see the patriot rear his banner high ;
    The troops march gaily through the busy town ;
Methinks I hear the trembling maiden sigh
    As her true knight goes forth to seek renown.
King Arthur, with his warriors brave and good,
    Comes forth, the dauntless flower of chivalry ;
And there be priests in monkish garb and hood,
    As well as motley fools of revelry.

'Neath walls of Troy I see the valiant Greek,
    Brave Ajax, and the mighty Hector there ;
In fancy hear the aged Priam speak,
    And see fair Helen with the golden hair ;
The war-like braves in single combat stand,
    The ponderous spear each doughty hero hurled,—
Fair Beatrice takes Dante by the hand,
    And shows the myst'ries of the hidden world.

    .   .   .   .

Sweet scenes of peace ! here in my native land
    These loving friends will each a posie bring,
With wooing words they take my ready hand,
    And lead, where meadows smile and brooklets sing ;
Where scented flow'rs cling round the cottage home,
    Sweet new-mown hay, and fields of ripening corn,—
The broad smooth lake, the gorge where waters foam,
    The shady grove, or by the scented thorn.
I see the fairies in the woody dells,
    I join their midnight revels on the green ;
The tower where the Enchanted Princess dwells,
    Embowered in a blaze of golden sheen.

With them I travel o'er the arid plain,—
    And wander where the palm and plantain grow,—
Through citron groves—or vine-clad summit gain,
    Climb mountains clad with thousand years of snow,

The heathy moor, and o'er the high hill top,
    And seem to breathe the cold crisp frosty air,
As from the lofty Alpine icy slope
    I see the fertile valleys stretching there.

'Mong lofty pines, or where the olives grow;
    Through far-off lands with Livingstone I roam,
Or loiter where the mighty rivers flow,
    While sitting in my easy chair at home.
There is no land in all the world we know,
    There is no mighty lake or frozen sea,
No hidden depth where foot of man can go,
    But my true friends will find and show to me.

For some will sing, and some will tell a tale,
    A simple story full of jocund glee,—
And anecdote with point that cannot fail
    To cheer the heart with true hilarity;
Kind jovial friends that merry songs can sing,
    Or with a touch of pathos bring the tear;
Anon I hear the wedding bells out-ring,
    And now for gallant deeds the sounding cheer.

Here true they stand, the many great and good,
    The fairest names the world can ever tell;
For some like gold the test of time have stood,
    And some!—Oh, there be "maidens fair" as well,
That take a foremost place amid the true,
    Good trusty friends there loitering by the wall;
Here Art and Poetry and Science too,
    With Travellers that come whene'er I call.

When day is done, with all its toil and care,
    The time that busy men together strove,—
My friends come forth the quiet hour to share,—
    The friends I trust, and trusting, best I love;
Here motley fool may preach a sermon true,
    Or sombre garb may tell a merry tale;
Here by the fire where these warm friendships grew
    They talk to me—the friends that never fail.

                              GEORGE DALZIEL.

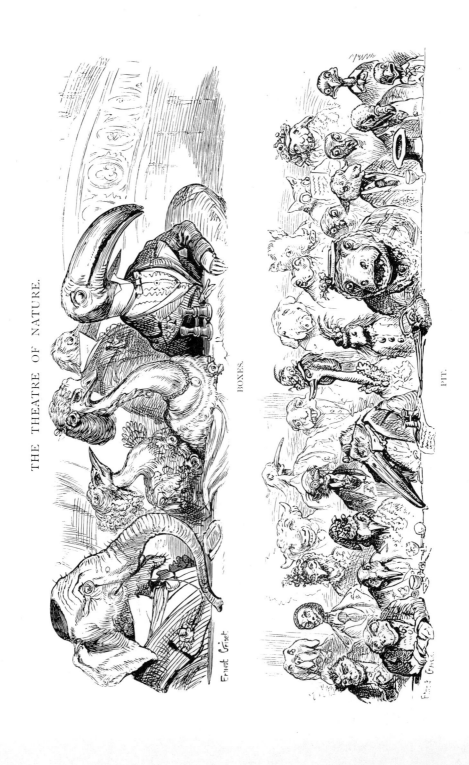

THE THEATRE OF NATURE.

BOXES.

PIT.

Ernest Griset.

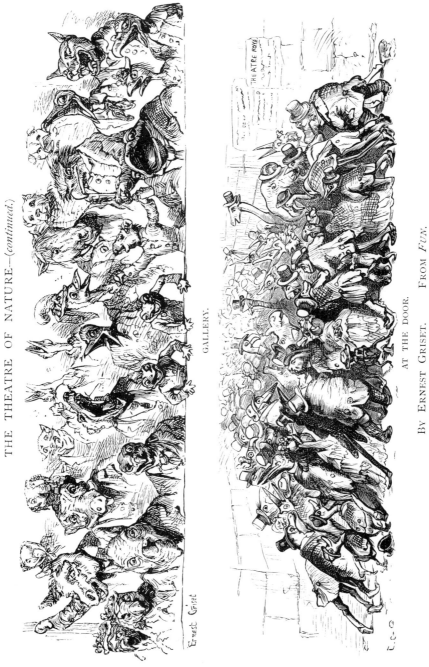

THE THEATRE OF NATURE.—(continued.)

GALLERY.

AT THE DOOR.

BY ERNEST GRISET. FROM FUN.

Ernest Griset

During the period that *Fun* was in our possession George Dalziel was a constant contributor, writing upon the passing events of the day under the general heading of " Dots by the Way."

Few matters in modern history caused greater excitement in the public mind than the many unsuccessful attempts of our troops to reach Khartoum for the relief of General Gordon, and, on the news of how the place had fallen and the brave hero had been murdered by a horde of savage Dervishes, the following verses appeared:

DEATH OF GENERAL GORDON.

[" The Fortress of Khartoum was treacherously delivered up to the Mahdi on January 26th, 1885, when General Gordon was slain."—*Daily Paper.*]

Hush! let no sound of revelry or song
    Be heard in all our busy streets to-day,—
For such dark news falls 'mong the surging throng
    As sends men sadly pondering on their way.
Sad news that sends a pang of crushing pain
    To every honest heart throughout the land.
Khartoum betrayed! her brave defenders slain,
    And Gordon fallen by the assassin's hand.

Great, noble Gordon, ever true and brave,
    That held this 'leagured city 'gainst the foe,—
And all that man could do, he did to save
    The women and their babes from direful woe;
But who can stand against the cunning art,
    The cruel, dark device, and darker sin
That traitors use, when with a fiendish heart
    They ope' the gates and let the foemen in?

Beloved by all who knew his noble heart,
    Or ever felt the warm grasp of his hand,
The loving kindness and the ready part
    He took in each good work in every land.

A gentle nature, kind as it was brave,
  To help the lowly in their poor estate,
He spent his life to free the fettered slave,
  And guide the suffering to a better fate

O grand career, unsullied to its close!
  Its splendour yet shall brighter shine, and tell
In glowing numbers how he faced his foes,
  And how by treason dire, great Gordon fell.
With head bowed down we mourn the good man gone,—
  And with our sorrow comes a sense of shame,
That in the midst of foes he stood alone,
  And died with added glory to his name.

The tale spreads like a black cloud o'er the land :
  'Tis like a darkening blight that falls at noon,
When men together meet and wondering stand,
  And gaze as though the stricken heart would swoon,—
The flaming sword, the "lightning of the spear,"
  Shone in the place where multitudes were slain,
The air is full of wailing, and we hear,
  Mingled with prayer, the groan of mortal pain.

GEORGE DALZIEL.

Again, when the decisive battle was fought under the command of Lord, then Sir Garnet, Wolseley, at Tel-el-Kebir, which practically brought the revolt led by Arabi Pasha to a close, this song appeared :

A SONG FOR OUR BRAVES.

[On the return of Troops from Egypt in 1882, after the victory at Tel-el-Kebir.]

A SONG now for the Guards,
  Right gallant deeds they've done,
And liberal rewards
  Their bravery has won ;
The world beheld with pride
  On Egypt's sandy plain
Their dreary midnight ride—
  The battle charge. Like rain
Before the raging storm they swept the foe away,
And victory was won at the dawning of the day.

There in the dull grey morn,
    With paling stars o'erhead,
We hear the bugle horn,—
    The shouts of those who led ;
We seem to hear the crash,
    To see the gleaming steel,—
The cannons roar and flash,
    The dusky foemen reel :
One moment at their guns they stood, then fled in
    wild dismay,
And victory was won at the dawning of the day.

Our heroes now come back,
    In pride they march along ;
Be sure they shall not lack
    Warm welcome, cheers and song ;
Tho' some were left behind,
    And fill a soldier's grave,
Their honoured names we'll find
    'Mong records of the brave
Who fell that morn while fighting and upheld old
    England's sway,
When victory was won at the dawning of the day.

                                    GEORGE DALZIEL.

For many years we published at intervals several small volumes of short stories, by George Dalziel, some of them having been previously printed in the various issues of the "Comic Annual." These volumes had considerable popularity, the most successful being, "My Neighbour Nellie," "Dick Boulin's Four-in-Hand," "The Story of a Shop," "A Soldier's Sweetheart," and "Only a Flower Girl." We also put together three volumes of verse, with the titles of "Mattie Grey, and Other Poems," "Faces in the Fire," and, later, "Unconsidered Trifles." The first two of these were printed exclusively for private distribution, but the last volume was addressed to

AN ILLOGICAL DE-DUCK-TION.   BY E. G. DALZIEL.   FROM *FUN*.

New Mother.—"Now then, Polly, come and have your hat on, there's a little duck!"
Polly.—"Shan't! Other little ducks don't wear none—there now."
[*The rest of the argument is lost in outcries and dissolved in tears.*]

U

the public through the publishing house of Mr.
Elliot Stock. Some few of the poems in each of
these volumes appeared originally in the pages of
the "Annual."

The following lines, printed in "Faces in the
Fire," were written as an affectionate tribute to the
memory of one of the sweetest and most loveable
of women :

MY MOTHER'S SONGS.

OF all the songs from sweetest voice,
　　In the sweet days of old,
That made my inmost soul rejoice,
　　However oft they're told,
Are those sweet songs my mother sung
　　While we were round her knee ;
When all the world seemed blythe and young
　　And fresh and fair to see.

O, I have wandered far away
　　In sunny lands of song,—
And I have heard the minstrels play
　　That thrilled the listening throng ;
Tho' sweet the charm when beauty sings,—
　　And sweet the minstrelsie,—
There is no charm that memory brings
　　Like those old songs to me.

Oft in the calm clear starry night,
　　Among the leafy trees,—
Or on the weird lone mountain height,
　　And in the gentle breeze,—
Or on the rough wild stormy sea,
　　When all is dark and drear,
The dear old songs will come to me,—
　　My mother's songs I hear.

Sweet is the strange enchanting spell
　　That lures all thought away,
To warm fireside or woody dell,
　　Where we were wont to play.

Around my boyhood's happy home
    Glad mem'ries fondly cling;
And oft' the sweet old songs will come
    My mother used to sing.

Through many years of joyous life
    I reach the sere and old;
Now all the battle and the strife,
    The fierce sun, and the cold,
Are o'er for me, and calm I wait
    Until the "joy-bells" ring;
For I shall hear at Heaven's gate
    My angel mother sing.

GEORGE DALZIEL.

Of the many art contributors, it will be sufficient if we state the names of the principal men whose works have adorned the pages of *Fun* and Hood's "Comic Annual." Of these, naturally, the cartoonists take the foremost place. Paul Gray, who held this position on Hood assuming the editorship, was a young Irish artist of very considerable promise, and displayed much fine feeling for black and white work. He also made drawings for some of our "Fine Art Books." He was a man of delicate constitution, and within twelve months of his joining the *Fun* staff he fell into a consumption and died. Shortly before the sad event, writing to us on other subjects, he said:

"I take the opportunity of saying how very pleased I am with the way in which the cartoons are engraved—some of the latter, more especially, could not possibly be better."

Jeffrey Prowse, in one of his poems, makes the following touching allusion to the early death of his young friend:

> " There is one of our band whom we cherished—
> 　The youngest, the purest, the best—
> In the frost of the night-time he perished,
> 　Going quietly home to his rest ;
> And we thought, as we buried our dear one,
> 　And mournfully turned us to go,
> That the summons was still sounding near one—
> 　　Listen ! *On bot,*
> 　　*On bot le rappel là-haut !* "

Then came W. J. Weigand, followed by A. Boyd Houghton. Notwithstanding the great ability of the latter, his quality of mind hardly fitted him to join in with Tom Hood's idea of the punctuality indispensable for conducting a weekly periodical. Next came Henry Doyle, a brother of the more famous Richard Doyle—an extremely careful and painstaking artist—who subsequently became Keeper of the Dublin National Gallery, with the distinction of C.B. After Doyle came Fred Barnard, an artist of surpassing versatility and humour. Perhaps it is not too much to say that in wit and true comicality he far outstripped all his predecessors on the journal ; but some slight difference of opinion with the editor—or was it some interference on the part of Mr. Wylam, the then proprietor—caused him to secede from the position. Then followed Gordon Thomson, an artist upon the merits of whose productions there was a wide difference of opinion ; but he did much good work —the series of double-pages in connection with the Franco-Prussian War being exceptionally strong. His large pictures for Christmas and other Holiday Numbers were remarkable for the varied topical

GOING HOME TO LOVE IN A COTTAGE.   BY F. A. FRASER.   FROM *FUN*.

THE very spot where the Snorkers held a pic-nic.   Oh! didn't the ladies cry out in one voice, "I could live in such a charming place for ever, if only ——"   At the self-same pic-nic, Tilbury Pawkins plighted his troth to Amelia Softispoon.   Now they are married, and Amelia has begun trying to live in the "charming place," and Pawkins is going home to a damp cottage and a rheumatic wife as blithely as a newly-married man should.

events he crowded into them, and those who remember his "Academy Skits" will know what quaint burlesques they were. Here is an appreciation by one of his most distinguished contemporaries :

Sir John Gilbert said :

"These funny 'Academy Skits' are extravagant to a degree, and at the same time they give such a complete embodiment of the picture in hand as to stamp the subject in my mind far more fixedly than any careful copy could possibly do."

Among the general contributors to *Fun* were many well-known draughtsmen—Professor H. von Herkomer, R.A.; George J. Pinwell, R.W.S.; Hal Ludlow, and "E. G. D." The last named (the eldest son of Edward Dalziel) was a young artist full of promise and great ability. Had he given continued attention to his oil painting he must undoubtedly have taken a very high position. He exhibited many pictures at the Royal Academy, the Grosvenor, and other galleries, but the allurement of black and white became too much for him, and he laid aside his brush for the pencil. He contributed many excellent works to our various "Fine Art Books," as well as to our "Bible Gallery." Unfortunately he died at the early age of 39. Amongst his many admirers was Sir John Gilbert, as the following letter, which refers to his drawings in *Fun,* will show :

"Vanbrugh Park, Blackheath,
"*20th December, 1878.*

"Dear Mr. Dalziel,—Pray accept my best thanks for your kind remembrance.

"The drawings as they appear weekly in *Fun* I always

ARGUMENTUM AD HOMINEM.   By J. MAHONEY.   FROM *FUN*.

Young Graceless.—"Natural selection!"   *Old Graceless.*—"Certainly! Only the finest specimens of the race survive."
Young Graceless.—"Come now, *that* won't do! Why, you're over sixty now, and good for another twenty years!"

admired. The *uncommon* humour, the wonderfully expressive faces, with attitude in accordance with the face, is always delightful and wonderful.

"The idea of gathering them together in a volume was excellent and I had intended to get the book. I thank you again for it.

"Pray remember me very kindly to your brother and your son, and with best wishes for your continued prosperity, health and happiness,

"I am, very truly yours,

"John Gilbert."

Among other artists employed on *Fun* were— William Small ; Harry French ; "F. A. F." (Francis A. Fraser), and his brother, G. Gordon Fraser, whose sketches of humorous Irish character were for several years a prominent feature in the journal (poor fellow! during the very severe winter of 1895 he was accidentally drowned while skating) ; E. J. Brewtnall, R.W.S., the water colour painter ; F. S. Walker, R.H.A. ; George Gatcombe, Harry Tuck ; and J. W. Houghton. The last named also contributed the dramatic criticisms, with illustrations, for several years. Jack Houghton is a ready writer of smart, clever verse, and wrote all the rhymed descriptions to Gordon Thomson's "Academy Skits."

Another very talented youth who it was our good fortune to introduce on *Fun's* pages, both in literature and art, was J. F. Sullivan. He was a student at South Kensington, when he first forwarded some sketches for our inspection ; and seeing they gave evidence of considerable ability, we at once availed ourselves of his drawings. Though he had much originality of conception and design, he did

OYSTERS.

"Here you are ! the finest natives ! best of appetite-creatives.
Come and buy ! Taste and try !"

By Ernest Griset.   From *Fun*.

not very readily acquire a "style" of his own,
such as is evidenced in his later productions.
Perhaps the most notable works Sullivan did were
some very clever character sketches—"The British
Working-man" and "The British Tradesman."   But
he was not an artist only, for, during the many
years he was associated with *Fun*, he contributed
to it a fair amount of very good verse and general
comic matter.

There was a distinct cleverness about the quaint
grotesque drawings of Ernest Griset, a young
Frenchman, who made his appearance in London

now many years ago. His drawings were at first exhibited in the window of a book shop close to Leicester Square, where they attracted considerable attention. Tom Hood had a great opinion of the artist's ability. They were generally in pen and ink, lightly tinted with delicate colour. We thought very highly of Griset's drawings, and soon enlisted his services, not only on *Fun* and " Hood's Annual," but upon many other publications—for which we bought hundreds of his drawings, and from them made selections. Tom Hood wrote clever verses to some of these, and we published them in book form through Messrs. Routledge as " Griset's Grotesques." We also got together several of his drawings which had appeared in *Fun* and published them as shilling books from the *Fun* Office.

Griset was, and is, a hard and rapid worker. He has been engaged in many other ways as an illustrator ; much on " Prehistoric Man." Also as a decorator of public halls, he has done good things.

W. S. Brunton, known as " Billy " Brunton, was a young Irishman full of racy humour and odd fancies. He was a constant contributor of comic sketches dealing with passing events of every-day life. It is well known that when the present Earl Dunraven was a young man he was occupied for many years as a journalist, on the London Press. He was of a genial disposition, a fluent writer, and a general favourite among his brethren of the pen, as well as a popular member of the Savage Club at the time that " Billy " Brunton and some few other kindred spirits kept the place

APROPOS TO A PROPOSAL.   BY HAL LUDLOW.   FROM *FUN*.

Frank (just accepted).—"Love thee, dearest? Ay, and when time shall have furrowed these youthful cheeks and dimmed the lustre of your eyes, when age shall have threaded silver amidst these glossy locks and bowed the figure erstwhile straight——"

Laura (hastily).—"Oh, Frank, I hope not! Think how old you will be!"

pretty lively with their jovial nights and merry Irish rollicking. On one occasion, shortly after Dunraven had come into the title and estates, a small group of " Savages " were standing gossiping in the club smoke-room, when he very quietly said :

" By the way, old chums, now that my position in the world is a little altered, and I have been obliged to change my name, I hope there may be no reserve on your parts, or change of feeling towards me, and that we shall continue to meet and chum together on precisely the same friendly terms, and with the same cordial good-fellowship, that has always existed among us."

" Billy " Brunton, who happened to be one of the group, laid his hand, with a caressing pat, on Dunraven's shoulder, and in an encouraging tone said :

"All right, old man, that shall be all right, so let your mind be entirely at ease on that score. Bedad, I pledge my word for it ; and I'm sure I speak the sentiments of every member of this club, that 'although your position in the world is a little altered, and you have been compelled to change your name,' you'll find no change in us—for you shall at all times be treated with precisely the same respect and the same consideration that has always been shown you here ; and to prove I'm entirely in earnest in what I say—gentlemen, I propose that Dunraven stands glasses round."

It is hardly necessary to say that the proposal met with approval by the entire party, or that it was responded to by the noble " Savage."

Henry Sampson remained editor of *Fun* and "Tom Hood's Comic Annual" for nearly four years, when he resigned that position to commence a weekly newspaper—the *Referee*.

Early in the Sixties we made the acquaintance of Edward Lear, who was a landscape painter of great distinction, a naturalist, a man of high culture, and a most kind and courteous gentleman. He came to us bringing an original chromo-lithographic copy of his "Book of Nonsense"—published some years before by McLean of the Haymarket. His desire was to publish a new and cheaper edition. With this view he proposed having the entire set of designs redrawn on wood, and he commissioned us to do this, also to engrave the blocks, print, and produce the book for him. When the work was nearly completed, he said he would sell his rights in the production to us for £100. We did not accept his offer, but proposed to find a publisher who would undertake it. We laid the matter before Messrs. Routledge & Warne. They declined to buy, but were willing to publish it for him on commission, which they did. The first edition sold immediately. Messrs. Routledge then wished to purchase the copyright, but Mr. Lear said, "Now it is a success they must pay me more than I asked at first." The price was then fixed at £120, a very modest advance considering the mark the book had made. It has since gone through many editions in the hands of F. Warne & Co.

Lear told us how "The Book of Nonsense" originated. When a young man he studied very much at the Zoological Gardens in Regent's Park. While he was engaged on an elaborate drawing of some " Parrots," a middle-aged gentleman used to come very frequently and talk to him about his work, and by degrees took more and more interest in him. One day he said, " I wish you to come on a visit to me, for I have much that I think would interest you." The stranger was the Earl of Derby. Lear accepted the invitation, and it was during his many visits at Knowsley that these " Nonsense" drawings were made, and the inimitable verses written. They were generally done in the evening to please the Earl's young children, and caused so much delightful amusement that he re-drew them on stone, and published them as before stated. That is how this clever, humorous book came into existence ; a work that will cause laughter and pleasure to young and old for all time. John Ruskin says of Lear's " Book of Nonsense" :

" Surely the most beneficent and innocent of all books yet produced is the ' Book of Nonsense,' with its corollary carols, inimitable and refreshing, and perfect in rhythm. I really don't know any author to whom I am half so grateful for my idle self as Edward Lear. I shall put him first of my hundred authors."

John Proctor, the celebrated cartoonist, had retired from his position, and had gone over to *Moonshine*, the then new " comic," and William Boucher had taken his place, before we became connected in any way with *Judy; or, The London Serio Comic Journal.* Charles H. Ross was the editor when the paper came into our hands in 1872.

MADAME.   BY FREDERICK BARNARD.

"*She is one of the most amiable ladies I ever met, and has a pleasant smile and a pretty something to say to one and all, and she doesn't mean a word she says.   Watch her now softly crossing the floor, no doubt fearful of waking old Mr. Topperton, whose heavy breathing might by the ill-disposed almost be likened to a snore.   See, she is carrying a pillow; doubtless it is to prop up Topperton's head, now resting against the hard wooden edge of the chair at a painful angle.   Not a bit of it.*"

"Behind a Brass Knocker" (*Judy*).—CHARLES H. ROSS

Published by Mr. Gilbert Dalziel.

He was a gifted writer of varied powers, a dramatist and novelist of the most sensational order. But above all, Ross was a great humorist, with a manner peculiarly his own. He was also a skilful draughtsman, and we engraved hundreds of his drawings. His pages of humorous pictures, which appeared in *Judy*, were generally signed " Marie Duval " (his wife's maiden name), and the subjects often savoured somewhat of French origin.

One of the principal contributors to the paper at this period was Ernest Warren, an admirable verse writer. He, too, wrote for the stage. Of his books, many of which were of " The Round Table " series, the most popular were " Four Flirts," and " The White Cat." Another, which had run through the Journal, and was written in collaboration with his friend Ross, was " Rattletrap Rhymes and Tootletum Tales." All three books went through many editions.

" The Bloomin' Flower of Rorty Gulch " was published in the last-named book, and shows Ross's power as a sarcastic verse writer. As a recitation, the poem is very popular, and in the hands of that clever and esteemed actor, E. J. Odell, who has made a feature of it for many years, it is highly appreciated in Bohemian and other circles.

In his " Book of Beauty " Ross says " On Love ":

" Ladies and gentlemen ! there is no such thing as love.

" This fact is thrown in by A. Sloper without any extra charge.

" Some people take a long while to find this out, and some never do quite find it out : those are the lucky ones.

" During A. Sloper's infancy, when A. Sloper was a mere

MISTER MITE.   BY FREDERICK BARNARD.

"'*What is it?*' *she asks.*
"'*It is* him—papa,' *responds Melia;* 'he has come back!'"

"Behind a Brass Knocker" (*Judy*).—CHARLES H. ROSS

Published by Mr. Gilbert Dalziel.

X

boy, he was under the impression that he was in love, and couldn't eat over two eggs and a couple of rashers for breakfast ; but it turned out he was wrong, and only wanted medicine.

"Later on he had another attack, and made poetry. He made a line that ended with *love*, and stuck *grove* on to the end of another, and *move* on to the end of a third, and *hove* and *stove* on to the end of the fourth and fifth, and still he was not happy, nor was any one else to whom he read the poem.

"Love has been the stock-in-trade of all poets ever since the first poet started in business, and they have generally treated the subject from a thoroughly business-like point of view.

"A young man once late at night told A. Sloper that some people never tell their love, but feed on their damask—and he fell down immediately after making the observation.

"A. Sloper has known men who could not make love, but have made boots, Geneva watches, and other things, very well indeed. He has also known men who could make love, but could never propose. You might have brought actions against them, and still they couldn't."

And see the glowing description of " The Beautiful Gymnast : A Fragment " :

" . . . Nothing could have been more lovely !

"Scarcely eighteen summers had passed over the golden-hued silkiness of the tightly-bound tresses of that classic head. The flush of health was on her peachy cheeks. The joyousness of youth lit up her big blue eyes, and wreathed her red lips into a smile, that showed two rows of glistening teeth. The tightly-fitting dress revealed in all its glorious young beauty the faultless contour of her form.

"She cast an eye of pardonable pride upon the shapely limbs supporting her ; then turned her eyes upward towards the horizontal bar, set her teeth, and jumped.

"An instant later, and she had sat down sharply on the resonant bounding-board with a deuce of a bump ! and all the plain young women looking on were smiling . . ."

One of the most interesting series of stories that Charles H. Ross wrote for *Judy*, he called ' Behind a Brass Knocker." This was done in conjunction

ON THE USELESSNESS OF NURSERY LORE. BY E. G. DALZIEL.

"NURSERY MORALS" (*JUDY*).

Published by Mr. Gilbert Dalziel.

with Fred Barnard, who made all of the drawings. It was rather a sad theme—the experiences of a lot of impecunious people living together in a boarding-house, the poorest of them all being Mrs. Mite, whose shifts and cunning ways are told with a touch of pathos, her crowning trouble being a drunken husband. The work had considerable success in volume form. Fred Barnard's work in this was of his very best kind.

Ross also wrote a series of wonderfully clever articles to accompany a set of drawings by E. G. Dalziel, which were strangely unlike the usual work of this artist—so much so, as to suggest the idea that he must have been under the influence of Gustave Doré at the time. Ross called them " Nursery Morals," which were of a fanciful character. After playfully rebuking " Little Bo-Peep" on her vanity, he concludes :

" I think the artist might as well have shown us the nose of one of the silly sheep peeping round a distant corner ; but perhaps the sheep were all tired of her airs and graces, and had taken themselves off in disgust. I am not naturally of a malignant disposition, but I sincerely trust she never did find those sheep. Don't you ? "

" On The Giant-Killer," he writes :

" I have every reason to believe that abnormally large men are comparatively harmless. There must be exceptions, of course, and I will give you 'Sir Roger' and Count Fosco. The Count, by the way, is a fictitious personage, and perhaps 'Sir Roger' was also rather that way inclined.

" These, however, were enormously fat men, not giants, and I have to do with giants. Now, we have it on good authority, that the intellect of a giant is generally as weak as his knees. We hear over and over again of giants in shows being awfully

On Love as a Passion.   By E. G. Dalziel.

"Nursery Morals" (Judy).

Published by Mr. Gilbert Dalziel.

bullied by the 'smallest man in the world,' who travels with him, and who is exhibited outside on the parade in a largish-sized doll's house, through the roof of which he pokes out his head, whilst he rings a bell from the second-floor window, and rests his feet in the front parlour."

He remarks "On the Utter Wrongness of Nursery Lore":

"The more I reflect upon the unworthiness of the Nursery hero, as compared with the spotless purity of my own character (I am a London tradesman), the more am I lost in wonder to think that these alarming humbugs should so long have been tolerated by an indulgent public. When I think of that fellow whose name is associated with the beanstalk of abnormal growth —an unhappy combination of rogue and fool—when I think of that wholesale murderer (another Jack), and indeed all the rest of them, I ask myself 'Why so?' and all that remains of the *Echo*, at one halfpenny, is discreetly silent."

"On Love as a Passion":

"The passion of love is very properly excluded from the subjects discussed in the best regulated nurseries. Indeed, in households where the young lady's material has reached a certain height and breadth and fulness, the love that has any particular amount of passion in it is not the one discussed. And I think it right that it should not be.

"Writing as I do exclusively for female babes (or rather, I should say, young lady babes, because a young lady babe ought not to be called a female, and would with reason feel annoyed at being called one), I am anxious to do away with the passion-ate love-fiction altogether. Of course, I know I have only to explain the thing properly, in my own particular way, and the thing will at once be done away with; and surely it is my duty to do so, when by doing so, I know I shall do good."

In 1888, Gilbert Dalziel, who had been working in the interests of the paper from the day it came into our hands, took over the journal, paying the sum of eight thousand pounds for it. He at

"Even Mr. Codlin had nothing to urge against a proposal so seasonable. Nelly, kneeling down beside the box, was soon busily engaged in her task, and accomplishing it to a miracle."

"The Old Curiosity Shop" (Household Edition).—CHARLES DICKENS.

By CHARLES GREEN, R.I.

By permission of Messrs. Chapman & Hall.

once made considerable alterations in the conduct
of the paper. Amongst his artistic staff were that
powerful draughtsman, W. G. Baxter; Bernard
Partridge, one of the most brilliant and deservedly
popular black and white men of our time; Maurice
Greiffenhagen, whose drawings had graced the pages
of *Judy* from the day of his early studentship;
Alfred Bryan, inimitable in his way; Fred Pegram,
Raven Hill, F. H. Townsend, and Fred Barnard.

With such a list of artists at work week by
week, small wonder that it should now be spoken
of as "The Golden Period" of *Judy*.

In the pages of *Judy*, Charles H. Ross created
the character of Ally Sloper and also of his friend
Ikey Moses. In the early part of 1884, Gilbert
Dalziel conceived and modelled a new publication,
to be called the *Half-Holiday*, in which Ally Sloper
was to be a leading character. It was finally decided, however, to add the Old Man's name to
the title, and on May 3rd, 1884, *Ally Sloper's
Half-Holiday* made its first appearance.

Amongst the many quaint features of the paper,
perhaps the "Award of Merit" stands foremost.
This decoration consists of a very clever design by
W. G. Baxter, executed in colours, and has been
presented to and accepted by men and women of
the highest distinction in all branches of art, science,
literature, music, and the professions generally.

Gilbert Dalziel has in his possession a collection
of autograph letters, in acknowledgment of the
"Award," from some of the most eminent folks
before the public during the latter part of the old

"'You're the wax-work child, are you not?' said Miss Monflather.
"'Yes, ma'm,' replied Nell, colouring deeply.'
'The Old Curiosity Shop" (Household Edition).—CHARLES DICKENS.

BY CHARLES GREEN, R.I.

By permission of Messrs. Chapman & Hall.

century, amongst whom may be mentioned—Lord Tennyson, as representing Literature; Sir John E. Millais, Bart., P.R.A., for Painting and Drawing on Wood; Sir Arthur Sullivan, for Music; Sir Charles Russell, for Law; Arthur W. Pinero and Sir Henry Irving, for the Drama; Lord Charles Beresford, for the Navy; and Lord Roberts (when he was in command in India), for the Army.

Charles H. Bennett was one of the most original artists of his period. Alas! his life was all too short. There was an individual stamp about his work— independent in manner and full of deep thought. We had many of his drawings through our hands and knew him well. A more earnest man concerning his work we never met; and, not unlike Pinwell, he held it as a principle that time should never be allowed to enter into the question; the task should be defined, but never trammelled by, "How long will it take?"—whether it be days, weeks or years, for the proper execution of the project. Perhaps his "Bunyan's Pilgrim's Progress" will rank as his greatest achievement.

We have already spoken of our connection with Messrs. Chapman & Hall, on that light feat of Doyle's, the "Panorama." There were also a very clever set of drawings for "Fairy Tales of all Nations," by Richard Doyle, and illustrations to Morley's "Oberon's Horn, and other Fairy Tales," by Charles H. Bennett, which we produced for the same firm.

When Charles Dickens abandoned the etchings

"*I made my way back to the 'Dolphin's Head.'   In the gateway I found J. Mellows looking at nothing, and apparently experiencing that it failed to raise his spirits.*

"*'I don't care for the Town,' said J. Mellows, when I complimented him on the sanitary advantage it may or may not possess; 'I wish I had never seen the Town.'*"

"The Uncommercial Traveller" (Household Edition).—CHARLES DICKENS.

BY E. G. DALZIEL.

By permission of Messrs. Chapman & Hall.

of H. K. Browne as a means of illustrating his books, the next work, " Our Mutual Friend," was placed in the hands of Marcus Stone, whose father, Mr. Frank Stone, A.R.A., had for many years been a next-door neighbour and a very constant friend of Dickens. Some of these drawings, which are marked with all the refinement and good taste of this popular artist, were entrusted to us to engrave.

We were early engaged on the various editions of the works of Charles Dickens, commencing (through our friend, Ebenezer Landells,) with the wood engravings for " Master Humphrey's Clock," which were soon followed by those for the " Christmas Books " from drawings by Richard Doyle, John Leech, and Daniel Maclise.

But by far the most important commission ever placed in our hands by Messrs. Chapman & Hall was the production and entire control of the illustrations for the Household Edition of the Works of Charles Dickens, which was commenced in serial form in 1871 and completed in 1879, thus extending over a period of eight years. The publishers began the issue with " Pickwick," using the original designs by H. K. Browne (" Phiz "), but immediately after this Mr. Frederick Chapman placed the entire control of the illustrations in our hands. We were to find the best artists we considered suitable for the various works. The first selected was James Mahoney, who had already attained some distinction in drawing on wood. He did in all three books, the first being " Oliver Twist," followed by " Little Dorrit " and "Our Mutual Friend." Mahoney

"*On the second occasion of my seeing him he said, huskily, to the man of sleep, 'Am I red to-night?'* '*You are,*' *he uncompromisingly answered.*"

'The Uncommercial Traveller" (Household Edition).—CHARLES DICKENS.

BY E. G. DALZIEL.

By permission of Messrs. Chapman & Hall.

had a firm, clear style of manipulation, and no one knew better than he how to make work look solid and firm by leaving large masses of white in his arrangement of colour. He painted some good water colours. We had several small examples, the most important of which is "A Bird of Prey," a repeat of one of his designs for "Our Mutual Friend." Charles Green, R.I., made a beautiful set of illustrations to "The Old Curiosity Shop." Every picture is carefully studied both as to character, scene, and subject; the picture of "Short and Codlin," with Nell and her Grandfather, being one of the most perfect. Green painted many very fine water colour pictures, several of which we were fortunate enough to possess.

"78 Park Road.

"Dear Mr. Dalziel,—These proofs are so beautiful I cannot find any fault; and should be a brute if I did. The only one I have touched is because it is a little too dark and heavy— perhaps it is a heavy proof. I am delighted with them generally. I send two more drawings. Please do not forget to let me have the three proofs I mentioned in this morning's letter.

"Yours very truly,

"C. Green."

Again on another occasion:

"I like those proofs very much indeed; they are beautiful. There is only one thing wants touching—the face of the Charwoman in No. 27 is rather muddy, it wants clearing up a bit. I have touched the proof."

H. French, a clever and popular artist, the son of an accomplished wood engraver, who came of the Bewick school, did the pictures for "Hard Times," and very good they were.

" *He stooped a little, and with his tattered blue cap pointed under the carriage. All his followers stooped to look under the carriage.*"

"A Tale of Two Cities" (Household Edition). CHARLES DICKENS.

BY FREDERICK BARNARD.

By permission of Messrs. Chapman & Hall.

F. A. Fraser, a well-known illustrator, made those for "Great Expectations."

A. B. Frost, an American artist of great ability, did "American Notes," and Gordon Thomson "Pictures from Italy." E. G. Dalziel undertook "Reprinted Pieces" and "The Uncommercial Traveller," as well as other short stories. Of "E. G. D.'s" work we will here quote two letters by distinguished artists in appreciation.

"2 Palace Gate,
"*30th January, 1878.*

"Dear Dalziel,—I ought to have thanked you for your kind and thoughtful present of Xmas books. The illustrations of your son to 'The Uncommercial Traveller' are *admirable.* I recognise his work in *Fun*, and the care of his work is not lost upon

"Yours very truly,

"J. E. Millais."

"Vanbrugh Park,
"Blackheath,
"*23rd December, 1877.*

"Dear Mr. Dalziel,—I thank you for the volume, where your son's drawings show an amazing care and truth—a certain weirdness most telling in some subjects, notably, 'Chips, the Carpenter'—the Devil with the Rat on his shoulder is *grand.* There is a Donkey, taken into custody by the police, most beautifully drawn. The Cart is by Albert Durer, so also is 'Mr. Baker's Trap'; 'A Cheap Theatre' is good, full of varied character; so is the Group of Chair-menders on title—the man's eyes screwed up because of the sun, and the woman looking through the back of the chair. There is a group of old women on p. 136 which is capital; very good character on p. 101, also on p. 84. 'Mr. J. Mellows,' p. 112, very good.

"With best wishes for health and happiness to you and yours,

"I am, dear Mr. Dalziel,

"Very truly yours,

"John Gilbert."

"'No matter! What do you mean, sir?' was the tart rejoinder.
'No matter! Do you think you bring your paltry money here as a
favour or a gift; or as a matter of business, and in return for value
received?'"

"Nicholas Nickleby" (Household Edition).—CHARLES DICKENS.

BY FREDERICK BARNARD.

By permission of Messrs. Chapman & Hall.

But of all the artists engaged on this edition Frederick Barnard held the most prominent position, he having fully illustrated no less than nine out of twenty books.

Barnard ranks as one of England's truly comic artists ; but he was not only comic, he was one of the most versatile artists of our time. He unquestionably stands among the foremost illustrators of Dickens. The many drawings he made for the Household Edition, as well as some larger pictures, illustrating the works of the great author, all possess a certain peculiarity : while the drawings are strictly in his own style, there is just enough resemblance to the figures created by H. K. Browne to save you a shock ; the Dick Swiveller, the Bill Sykes, and other characters are the same as one had accepted when the stories were first written.

A powerful set of drawings are those for "How the Poor Live," which were commissioned by Gilbert Dalziel, in connection with G. R. Sims' articles, for publication in the *Pictorial World.*

Again, how grand are many of his designs for the "Pilgrim's Progress," which we prepared for Alexander Strahan ; one of the most effective is "Lord Hategood," from which we commissioned him to paint an oil picture. Barnard was no mean painter : perhaps his "Saturday Night in the East End" and "The Guards' Band Marching" are amongst his most important works. He also painted a "Ball-room Scene," of an elegant character, from one of the Dickens' books, that had a very prominent place in the Institute of Painters in Oil Colours.

Our long connection with Barnard was of close intimacy and friendship; he was a delightful companion, amusing, and full of bright repartee, and would often "set the table in a roar."

As a mimic and comic singer he was inimitable. A favourite song of his at studio evenings was "I Long to be a Hartist, Mother," written by himself, we believe, and screamingly funny. As a practical jokist, Fred Barnard was simply *au fait*. On one occasion he called at Soane's Museum in Lincoln's Inn Fields, and asked the porter if Sir John Soane was at home. "Why, lor bless you, sir," said the man, "Sir John Soane has been dead these sixty years." Barnard was staggered at the news and overwhelmed with grief, and beating his breast he cried, "Dead! Dead! Dead! And we were boys at school together!"

His own death, poor chap, was tragic, and a great shock to all who knew him. He was an ardent smoker. One morning, having had breakfast in bed, he requested that he should not be disturbed again for some hours; when the servant went to call him there was no response, and on the door being forced open the room was found to be full of smoke, the bed-clothes smouldering fire. It is supposed that while courting further sleep he lit a pipe, which, falling from his mouth, ignited the clothes; although somewhat severely burnt, his death was, in fact, due to suffocation, and he passed away while in a state of insensibility.

George Dalziel
1901

FROM A PHOTOGRAPH BY GRACE AND DORA DALZIEL.

Edward Dalziel

1907

Thomas BGS Dalziel, '1901

OUR PUPILS.

—◆—

EARLY in the year 1844 we took our first pupil, Francis Fricker, a very steady, industrious fellow, who was always punctual and reliable. He became a good engraver, and remained with us, without intermission—with the exception of two or three weeks' holiday in each year, which we made a practice of giving to all our pupils—until we broke up our establishment in 1893.

Being all draughtsmen ourselves, we did not take pupils specially for engraving alone ; although, from our earliest days, we made it a rule to place any commission that was intrusted to us in the hands of the best artists we could find, whose peculiar ability suited them for the subject in question.

Nevertheless, we established a school to teach our pupils drawing. We got together a good collection of plaster casts—the best obtainable ; also other matter suitable for study from the flat and round ; works on "Anatomy," on " Beauty," and on " Perspective." We also provided all the materials for working free of cost. The engraver's day at that time was a long one — nine hours — and the drawing only began after the day's work had been finished ; and to this, perhaps, is due the fact that all did not avail themselves of what had been planned for them. The pupils who did attend the meetings, and who doubtless possessed the stronger love of art, benefitted to no small extent.

Among those who availed themselves of these advantages were Harry Fenn and Charles Kingdon, two of our earliest and very cleverest pupils. Soon after they completed their term with us they took ship to Canada, having determined to visit the principal cities there and in the United States of America. This they did, settling in New York City, where they soon found profitable employment.

Harry Fenn took at once to drawing on wood and water colour painting, making very rapid progress in both branches of art, and soon becoming the most popular landscape draughtsman in America. It was he who projected, planned, and made all the drawings for " Picturesque America." It came about in this way. He was dining with the well-known publisher, D. Appleton, who, during conversation, regretted that America did not afford such fine material for landscape art as the Old Country—that there was, in fact, nothing picturesque in America. Fenn said : " Give me the chance and you shall see what a variety of beautiful material you have got in America." The reply was : " Well, you shall have a try if you like. Do a few drawings and let us see." Fenn made a few drawings, which encouraged the publisher to carry out the idea ; and he did a work which was, perhaps, one of the most brilliantly successful illustrated books ever published, and the forerunner of several similar works, all of which were filled with beautiful examples of his skilful pencil. He still continues to be a popular black and white artist, but devotes much time to painting in water colours.

Joseph Pennell, in his "Modern Illustration," says, "Henry Fenn's illustrations to 'Picturesque America' entitle him to be called the Nestor of his Guild, not only for the delicacy, truth and refinement of his drawing, but also because of the enormous success of the publication."

Charles Kingdon, by far the best engraver of the two, was also very popular in America, but he was of a restless nature and had not the persistent industry of his companion. He died young, and in his death the world lost a brilliant young artist. He married an American lady soon after settling there, and it is worthy of mention, so we have been told, that his daughter, who evidently inherited her father's art instincts and good looks—for Kingdon was a very handsome fellow—was a popular member of the celebrated Augustin Daly's company, and became the wife of an American millionaire.

Another of the most industrious and constant workers was George G. Kilburne, who, soon after completing his engagement with us, gave up engraving altogether and took to painting—mostly in water colours—in which he has long held a prominent position in the Royal Institute of Painters in Water Colours, as well as being a very frequent exhibitor at the Royal Academy. He was one of the most satisfactory pupils we ever had. He took up engraving with great aptitude, and from the day he came to us his work was always good. Only the second drawing given to him to work upon was so perfect, that it was published with the set to which it belonged. A peculiarity with Kilburne was that if he were asked to do anything, you found him doing it immediately; with him no time was wanted for preparation. Though he left our studio and forsook the branch of art we taught him, our connection, instead of being severed, became the closer by his marrying the elder daughter of our late brother Robert.

Charles A. Ferrier, a young Scotchman of varied capabilities, who had made some small efforts at wood engraving in his native town of Arbroath, without instruction, came to us to seek employment through an introduction he had obtained to William Harvey. He was a youth of considerable promise and full of enthusiasm for his art. Though the specimens he had to show were very crude, he had evidently been looked upon as a genius by his Scottish friends; but on entering our studio he was indefatigable in his studies, and eager for improvement. Before he had been two months with us he became London correspondent to an Arbroath weekly paper. This letter he generally knocked off during the hour allowed for dinner in the middle of the day. We have reason to believe he turned his attention very much to scientific subjects, and became a Fellow of more than one of the learned Societies. During the whole of his life he has been a staunch teetotaler, and has worked hard in the temperance cause. He became the personal friend of George Cruikshank, Dr. Richardson, and many scientific people, who preferred him as an engraver because of the knowledge he possessed of the objects he had to work upon. Taken altogether, Ferrier became one of the most remarkable men who had their beginning in our studio.

"W. Y.," a pupil whose name for obvious reasons we will not give, came to us when about nineteen years of age. He was a member of a good county family—a younger son; he had good taste for art and some skill as a draughtsman. By the wish of his elder brother, he was put with us to learn engraving. His development in our art was simply wonderful, his manipulative power was quite extraordinary; it was the one case in our experience where it seemed as if the pupil had come to teach the masters. He was steady, punctual to his long day's work, and in every way exemplary, a gentleman in manner, and a great favourite with all the assistants and other pupils; but it was known to his fellow-workers that at a certain date he was to come into a considerable sum of money, and he had often said that when he got it, "then farewell to industry, to art, and to respectability." His words were: "When I get it I will let fly." And, sad to relate, he did "let fly." He had been working out of our studio for some two or three months, when he suddenly disappeared, and the last we heard of him was that he was spending his time,

and his money chiefly in the immediate vicinity of
the Surrey Theatre, and that in an adjacent public-
house bar he was seen lighting his pipe with a five
pound note. Poor fellow! It was the old, old story
—the drink—the drink that did it.

Alexander Aitcheson Dalziel and John Sanderson
Dalziel, the two sons of our brother Robert, also,
on leaving school, became pupils to learn wood
engraving. The elder brother, Alexander, shortly
after completing his term, married and went out
to South Africa, where for a time he coupled
scholastic work with his engraving ; but after a bit
he gave up art altogether and went on with his
teaching only—while John emigrated to America, and
settled down in Philadelphia for many years, where
he executed a large number of elaborate, highly-
finished works, chiefly of a scientific character, much
of which has been reproduced in this country. At
the time we write he is turning his attention to
fruit culture in Colorado.

A. W. Bayes was introduced to us by H. Stacy
Marks, R.A., as a young man who had been
engaged as a draughtsman at some manufacturing
works in the country, and had shown a wonderful
capacity for design. We could not say he came
to us as a pupil ; but whatever progress he made in
our studio was the result of the practice derived from
the subjects given to him, and owing to the advantage of his seeing a great variety of drawings by
the leading artists of the time. He was very in

dustrious and very rapid. He worked with us for
many years, until, for the further development in
painting and other branches of his art, he found
it an advantage to have a place of his own. With
us he had illustrated a number of children's books,
the most important being the works of Hans
Christian Andersen, for which he made a very
large number of drawings. These books went
through many editions. He also made a set
of drawings from Bible history, and another set
from the New Testament, all of which were
published for us by Messrs. Routledge, Warne &
Co., with a fair amount of success. Bayes for
some years has devoted himself almost entirely to
painting in oil, and has produced many important
works—chiefly of a historical order.

Phil Ebbutt came to us on the recommendation of
our friend George R. Sims. He had a natural taste
for drawing, and was quick at design. He worked
much on our publication, *Jack and Jill*, including
political cartoons, and romances strictly historical.
He also made many drawings for *Fun*, which were
mostly of a social character. In all he was an industrious, willing worker, but his progress was hindered
by an affection of the eyes, which now and again
demanded complete rest; though that, for a time,
was got over and he went to work again. He
also made many drawings as book illustrations, and
was one of the original artists on the *Daily Graphic*,
working for the first number of that journal. But
the eye trouble again caused him to terminate so

close a connection, and he continued as an occasional contributor only.   He still holds a prominent place as a journalistic artist, doing much good work.

Hal Ludlow as a boy showed great taste and skill in drawing.   His friends wished him to be a wood engraver and placed him with us as an apprentice for that purpose; but he made little or no progress in that branch and was soon put to drawing entirely, and very quickly developed as a clever designer.   He made hundreds of drawings for children's and other books; some of the former were carried out in colours—what are generally known as "Toy Books."   He soon became an expert in pure pen and ink work, and when the *Pictorial World* was under our control, made a large number of careful drawings of social life—many of every-day events, notably river and race scenes.   He also made many important drawings of theatrical representations—new plays, opera and music hall subjects.   His work had become so popular that Mason Jackson came to us on behalf of the *Illustrated London News*, to know if we would allow Ludlow to make drawings on wood for that journal, saying, "it was a pity that such clever drawings should all be reproduced by process," which he regarded as an inferior manner of rendering them. What a change has come since that period!   How completely has the then-thought "superior" manner had to stand aside for the "inferior"!   We may here state that, in the long past, we always thought that some automatic process would be perfected for the proper reproduction of point work, or what was always known as "facsimile" drawing. Of Ludlow's work as a popular designer and painter, it is not necessary to speak further than to say that his smaller water colours rival in grace and minute finish the work of Jan Van Beers.

George Gatcombe was a companion and friend of Phil Ebbutt, and through that fact came to us. He showed an early taste for drawing, was from the first a very rapid workman, and soon developed to an extent that made his work suitable for publication. We gave him an opportunity by the introduction of his work on *Fun*, in which he evinced a distinct capacity for the elegant in his social pictures. He made many illustrations for books; and did much at various times for "Hood's Annual." Some of his political cartoons, too, showed a distinct taste in that direction. He also produced several designs of a historical character. Gatcombe is a good all-round black and white artist.

Among the many other pupils and assistants who have passed through our studios, and proved themselves steady and accomplished artists, we must not omit to mention Harry Leighton, E. J. Wallis, who has lately turned his attention very successfully to landscape photography, Walter Williams, William Arrowsmith, and James Clark, who, like his fellow-pupil Frank Fricker, remained with us for over forty years.

THE PRINTING OFFICE.

———◆———

With the object of printing our own " Fine Art
Books," early in the year 1857 we decided to set up
a small printing office, which necessitated our ob-
taining much more extensive accommodation than
we at that time possessed. We secured a long
lease of the premises, 110—at that time known as
53—High Street, Camden Town, and under the
style and title of The Camden Press gradually
built up a large printing and publishing business.
During nearly forty years of varied experience in
this branch of the business, we printed a great
number of important works for other publishers, as
well as our own. Amongst the very last of these
was " Dalziel's Bible Gallery."

The Camden Press, where this book was printed,
is now in the hands of Charles and Harvey Dalziel.
It fully maintains its repute for high-class art work,
after the manner of the old firm, but "running to
numbers" such as were never dreamt of in the
days of

Dalziel Brothers

LIST OF

FINE ART AND OTHER ILLUSTRATED BOOKS

PRODUCED BY AND UNDER THE ENTIRE SUPERINTENDENCE
OF THE BROTHERS DALZIEL.

———◆◆———

DATE	SUBJECT.	ILLUSTRATED BY	PUBLISHED BY
1850	PILGRIM'S PROGRESS	William Harvey	*David Bogue.*
,,	HOME FOR THE HOLIDAYS ...	Kenny Meadows	*J. Cundall.*
1851	JACK THE GIANT KILLER ...	Richard Doyle	*Cundall & Adey*
..	AN OVERLAND JOURNEY TO THE GREAT EXHIBITION OF 1851	,, ...	*Chapman & Hall.*
1852	THE SALAMANDRINE ...	Sir John Gilbert, R.A., P.R.W.S. ...	*Ingram & Cook.*
1854	KRUMMACHER'S FABLES ...	J. R. Clayton	*Nathaniel Cook.*
,,	ORIENTAL FAIRY TALES ...	William Harvey	*Chapman & Hall.*
1856	LONGFELLOW'S POEMS ...	Sir John Gilbert, R.A., P.R.W.S. ...	*G. Routledge & Co.*
1857	POETS OF THE 19TH CENTURY	Various Artists	,,
,,	DRAMATIC POEMS OF BARRY CORNWALL	,, ...	*Chapman & Hall.*
,,	BRYANT'S POEMS	,, ...	*Appleton, New York.*
1858	HOME AFFECTIONS OF THE POETS	,, ...	*G. Routledge & Co.*
,,	GERTRUDE OF WYOMING ...	,, ...	,,
,,	MILTON'S COMUS	,, ...	,,
,,	BEATIE'S MINSTREL	Birket Foster	,,
,,	SUMMER TIME IN THE COUNTRY	Various Artists	,,
,,	LIFE OF CHRIST, AND THE MIRACLES	F. R. Pickersgill, R.A.	*Chapman & Hall*
,,	FAIRY TALES (H. MORLEY) ...	C. H. Bennett	,,
,,	OTTO SPECTER'S PICTURE FABLES	Otto Specter	*Routledge, Warnes & Routledge.*
1859	OBERON'S HORN (H. MORLEY)	C. H. Bennett	*Chapman & Hall.*
,,	WORDSWORTH'S POEMS ...	Various Artists	*Routledge, Warnes, & Routledge.*
,,	ODES AND SONNETS	Birket Foster	,,
,,	MILES STANDISH ...	Sir John Gilbert, R.A., P.R.W.S. ...	,,
1860	MONTGOMERY'S POEMS ...	Various Artists	,,
,,	ELIZA COOK'S POEMS ...	,, ...	,,
1858 to 1861	SHAKESPEARE'S WORKS (3 Vols.)	Sir John Gilbert, R.A., P.R.W.S. ...	,,
1861	ORLEY FARM	Sir J. E. Millais, P.R.A.	*Chapman & Hall.*
,,	LALLA ROOKH	Sir John Tenniel	*Longman & Co.*

z

DATE.	SUBJECT.	ILLUSTRATED BY	PUBLISHED BY
1861 to 1863	WOOD'S NATURAL HISTORY & WOOD'S NATURAL HISTORY OF MAN (5 Vols)... ...	Various Artists	*Routledge, Warne, & Routledge.*
1861 and 1862	BIRDSEYE VIEWS OF SOCIETY	Richard Doyle	*Smith, Elder & Co.*
1862	PICTURES OF ENGLISH LAND-SCAPE	Birket Foster	*Routledge, Warne, & Routledge.*
,,	ENGLISH SACRED POETRY ...	Various Artists	
,,	FRAMLEY PARSONAGE ...	Sir J. E. Millais, P.R.A. ...	*Smith, Elder & Co.*
1863	PILGRIM'S PROGRESS ...	J. D. Watson, R.W.S.	*Routledge, Warne, & Routledge.*
1864	PARABLES OF OUR LORD ...	Sir J. E. Millais, P.R.A.	,,
,,	ROBINSON CRUSOE	J. D. Watson, R.W.S.	,,
,,	THE SMALL HOUSE AT ALLINGTON	Sir J. E. Millais, P.R.A.	*Smith, Elder & Co.*
,,	DALZIEL'S ARABIAN NIGHTS	Various Artists	*Ward & Lock.*
,,	THE GOLDEN HARP	,, ...	*Routledge, Warne, & Routledge.*
1865	DALZIEL'S GOLDSMITH ...	G. J. Pinwell, R.W.S. ...	*Ward & Lock.*
,,	ALICE IN WONDERLAND ...	Sir John Tenniel	*Macmillan & Co.*
,,	HOME THOUGHTS ...	A. Boyd Houghton, R.W.S. ...	*Routledge, Warne, & Routledge.*
,,	AN OLD FAIRY TALE ...	Richard Doyle	,,
,,	PILGRIM'S PROGRESS	Thomas Dalziel...	*Ward & Lock.*
1866	DON QUIXOTE	A. Boyd Houghton, R.W.S. ...	*F. Warne & Co.*
,,	WORDSWORTH'S POEMS FOR THE YOUNG...	J. Pettie, R.A., and J. MacWhirter, R.A.	*A. Strahan & Co.*
,,	THE SPIRIT OF PRAISE ...	Various Artists	*F. Warne & Co.*
,,	GRISET'S GROTESQUES ...	Ernest Griset	*G. Routledge & Sons.*
1867	A ROUND OF DAYS	Various Artists	,,
,,	GOLDEN THOUGHTS	,, ...	*F. Warne & Co.*
,,	JEAN INGELOW'S FABLES ...	,, ...	*Longman & Co.*
1868	NORTH COAST POEMS (ROBT. BUCHANAN)...	,, ...	*G. Routledge & Sons.*
1869	WAYSIDE POSIES	,, ...	,,
,,	BALLAD STORIES OF THE AFFECTIONS... ...	,, ...	,,
,,	KRILOF FABLES	A. Boyd Houghton, R.W.S. ...	*A. Strahan & Co.*
,,	RHYME AND REASON ...	Various Artists	*G. Routledge & Sons.*
1870	LEAR'S BOOK OF NONSENSE	Edward Lear	,,
,,	OUR NATIONAL NURSERY RHYMES	Various Artists	*Novello, Ewer & Co.*
1871	THROUGH THE LOOKING GLASS	Sir John Tenniel	*Macmillan & Co.*
,,	CHRISTMAS CAROLS ...	Various Artists	*Novello, Ewer & Co.*
1872	SING SONG (CHRISTINA ROS-SETTI)	Arthur Hughes	*G. Routledge & Sons.*
1874	PICTURE POSIES	Various Artists	,,
,,	SUNLIGHT OF SONG	,, ...	*Novello, Ewer & Co.*
1877	ART RAMBLES IN THE ISLANDS AND HIGHLANDS OF SCOT-LAND	J. T. Reid	*G. Routledge & Sons.*

DATE.	SUBJECT.	ILLUSTRATED BY	PUBLISHED BY
1877	ARABIAN NIGHTS ENTERTAINMENT	Thomas Dalziel	*G. Routledge & Sons.*
1871 to 1879	DICKENS'S HOUSEHOLD EDITIÓN	Various Artists	*Chapman & Hall.*
1880	PILGRIM'S PROGRESS	,, ...	*A. Strahan & Co.*
,,	DALZIEL'S BIBLE GALLERY...	,, ...	*G. Routledge & Sons.*
1880	BYGONE MOODS (J. T. JUDKIN)	,, ...	*Longman for J. T. J.*
1883	RHYME AND REASON (LEWIS CARROL)	A. B. Frost	*Macmillan & Co.*
1885	A TANGLED TALE (LEWIS CARROL)	,, ...	,,

FINE ART BOOKS

PARTLY THE WORK OF THE BROTHERS DALZIEL.

DATE.	SUBJECT.	ILLUSTRATED BY	PUBLISHED BY
1841	POEMS AND PICTURES ..	Various Artists	*J. Burns.*
1841 to 1846	WAVERLEY NOVELS (ABBOTSFORD EDITION)	,, ...	*T. Cadell.*
1849	THE KING OF THE GOLDEN RIVER	Richard Doyle	*Smith, Elder & Co.*
,,	FAIRY TALES OF ALL NATIONS	,, ...	*Chapman & Hall.*
,,	A JAR OF HONEY FROM MOUNT HYBLA	,, ...	*Smith, Elder & Co.*
1854	TUPPER'S PROVERBIAL PHILOSOPHY	Various Artists	*Hatchard & Co.*
,,	THE POETICAL WORKS OF GEORGE HERBERT ...	,, ...	*J. Nisbet & Co.*
1857	TENNYSON'S POEMS	,, ...	*Moxon & Co.*
,,	POLLOCK'S COURSE OF TIME	,, ...	*Blackwood & Co.*
1858	LAYS OF THE HOLY LAND...	,, ...	*J. Nisbet & Co.*
,,	THE BOOK OF JOB	Sir John Gilbert, R.A., P.R.W.S.	,,
1859	THOMPSON'S SEASONS ...	Various Artists	,,
1863	LAYS OF THE SCOTTISH CAVALIERS	Sir J. Noel Paton, P.R.S.A., and H. Waller Paton	*Blackwood & Co.*
1864	INGOLDSBY LEGENDS	J. Leech, G. Cruikshank and Sir John Tenniel	*R. Bentley.*

INDEX.